MY DEEPEST HEART'S DEVOTIONS 5

AN AFRICAN WOMAN'S DIARY - BOOK 5

GERTRUDE KABATALEMWA

Edited by NONA BABICH AND TERESA SKINNER

Photography by ALISA ALBERS

Photography by TERESA SKINNER

ISBN: 978-1-950123-19-3

Copyright © 2019 by Teresa Skinner

Unless otherwise indicated, all Scripture quotations are taken from the Holy Bible, King James Version - Public Domain Scripture quotations marked (ESV) ® Bible (The Holy Bible, English Standard Version®), copyright © 2001 by Crossway, a publishing ministry of Good News Publishers. Used by permission. All rights reserved."

Scripture quotations marked (NIV) are taken from the Holy Bible, New International Version®, NIV®. Copyright © 1973, 1978, 1984, 2011 by Biblica, Inc.™ Used by permission of Zondervan. All rights reserved worldwide. www.zondervan.com The "NIV" and "New International Version" are trademarks registered in the United States Patent and Trademark Office by Biblica, Inc.™

All rights reserved.

No part of this book may be reproduced in any form or by any electronic or mechanical means, including information storage and retrieval systems, without written permission from the publisher, except for the use of brief quotations in a book review.

Gone so soon,
with all the dedicated work she had done...
we will continue with the work she has left behind.
showing people "God's Love and Care"
Emmanuel Mwesigye

CONTENTS

Foreword   xi

1. Ruggadization   1
2. Con Tu Amor   5
3. Wedding of Princess of Tooro   9
4. Baptism of Trials   11
5. Still My Heart is at Rest   15
6. God's Saints are Not Instantly Made   21
7. You Do Not Know Me   27
8. Discovery, Life of Yourself, Serendipity   33
9. Two Dreams   39
10. Change a "No" Face to a "Yes" Face   41
11. My Other Name is Kabatalemwa Tigalyoma   45
12. Keep Loving God, He Will Live   49
13. The Day I Will Walk to Heaven   57
14. People Lose the Joy of Life   59
15. Just Enough Truth With Falsehood   63
16. Jesus is the Reason Why I Live   75
17. Opportunity to Give… So That He Can Bless Them   79
18. Trials Are Coming to People of God in a Whirlwind   85
19. Holy Spirit Prepare Us for the Marriage Supper   89
20. "Komukituurukye"   93
21. All I want is you Jesus   97
22. Store Your Riches Where No Rats… Can Get Them   101
23. Six Things To Pray For   105
24. Our Lives are Worthless Without God   109
25. Reorganizing Our Inner Man   113
26. The Only Faithful Friend Is Our Lord   119
27. The Religious Spirit   125
28. Only You with Your Love   131

About the Author

WORD OF THE LORD FOR GERTRUDE KABATALEMWA

I believe I heard the Lord say
You are a General - in His army
You are a woman of valor
You are a woman of great faith
Those who have preceded you and those that will follow

There is not one with a greater faith as you
You are an Apostle - there will be more churches established
Training up those in your care now to begin other church groups
As His message of salvation and love continues to be spread
throughout the nation

I believe I heard the Lord say
Your job is not done
You have accomplished much but
There is much more to be accomplished
He has given you a great vision
And those to stand with you in bringing forth this vision
You cannot do this alone

I believe I heard Him say
Begin to seek Him
There are those who are now working in various projects
But He will begin to show you - one by one-
Those whom He will raise up to walk beside you
To further along and to fulfill the vision
Walking with you in unity, harmony and one accord
To accomplish the same vision He has given you
You to delegate responsibility for various projects to those He shows you
So that you can be freed up to begin new endeavors
And to further along others

Multiplication - multiplication of help - more people to be set in place to help you
To take on more of the work that needs to be done
Delegation - your delegating more work to others to free up yourself

He will continue to provide for you
Finances help in all you need
The vision is expanding
More will be started
More will be accomplished

And I believe I hear the Lord say
The angels of the Lord encamp around you
And continue to be at your side
To protect you and provide for the needs
Rest in peace knowing that even greater things are in store
Greater things will be accomplished

And I believe I hear the Lord say

You have been found faithful
He loves you very much

And the Lord says to you
"Well done My good and faithful servant!"

Sunday Mar 28, 2010 Approximately 5:20 PM

FOREWORD

We may not agree with what Ms. Gertrude Kabatalemwa has written. It may not be politically correct for our generation. But, let us get passed our judgements, and hear the heart of this African woman.

If so, we will find ourselves understanding a depth of spirituality that will most likely be lost to the next generations.

AFRICA HAS SOMETHING TO SAY TO US.

May we listen intently with raw ears to hear a direction that could keep our future from becoming sterile.

Teresa Skinner
All Nations International

CHAPTER ONE
RUGGADIZATION

GOD CANNOT BE PUSHED, cannot be bribed, cannot be Manipulated, cannot be hurried, He comes, and works at His own timing.

It is the eve of 15th November to complete two years since 15th November 2010 when I finished 45 days of water and honey fast. Since Monday 12th I have been suffering with malaria which brought on diarrhea and vomiting. This day I could not make it to the office because I was so weak. Emma took the van to be repaired and look for tyres to make it ready to go to the village. Around 6.00pm I asked myself Lord when I finished the 45 days fast, I thought you were going to immediately start using me tremendously, spiritually, physically or materially; but now it is two years gone. In my spirit I started preaching myself. Our God does not come early or come late He comes right in time. The things of God make me wonder at times, His answers come like a big bang. that is suddenly. At times they come slowly as they unfold like a beautiful flower. For example, a rose flower, it brings a bud, when you smell on the bud, the sweet scent is not there, it is closed inside. After some days it starts opening slowly, first the green cup, then petals one by one start shooting out until when the whole flower opens up, there you can smell the sweet scent. So God's answers do not come as we expect them. We human beings, we always want our answers there and then, but it is not with our God. He takes time to prepare what is appropriate for His child. He first puts it together, presses it and shakes it to fit into our surroundings. Maybe I will liken it with a computer ruggadization. That before a computer is approved it has to go through a test which is called ruggadization. First it is put into a freezing point and it stays there for a day and next it is placed into an extreme hot place also it stays there for a day, and lastly it is driven on a rugged road where the shaking is at the extreme. When it comes out still functioning without any defects it has passed the ruggadization test and then it can be given a guarantee. All these tests proves that if this computer is taken to a place like Alaska or Iceland where it is very cold it will survive, when it is taken to Sahara or Mohave Desert it will stand the heat, and lastly when it is taken on to the rugged potholed roads in Africa still it will hold together. So does our God, before He gives you a bang of a miracle or when He opens you, petal by petal you will not soar with pride or start familiarizing Him. This has happened so many times with Christian music artists. After giving them songs and lyrics to help His people through music the ones He has given those songs, they start calling them their songs and start trading with them. When they are called to minister, they ask the church or group inviting them to pay, the one who pays the highest is where they go. And worse still they take the songs given to them by God and offer them on the altars of satan the pentagram in the name of launching, dress in the worldly manner for Pam Award, flashing satanic signs of the goatee. Pastors go on competition of biggest church, the loudest music, the biggest houses and big cars. They create services for lunch hour, evening glory, 5 o'clock on Wednesday, 31st December all open grounds are booked one year in advance and if you buy so many CDs of my music you enter a raffle to win a car gambling, pastors grade counseling prayers according to amount of money one puts in an envelope. Therefore, Our Father first ruggadizes those whom He is to use in His ministry, but some of those jump the ruggadization because time is running out for them to go to make money. That is why there are many meaningless churches. Some dodge the ruggedization

because it is to cold, yet for others when it is too hot or too bumpy, will they will not stand it. You find them jumping out and running to start a church prematurely when they have failed God's ruggadization tests. We need to wait patiently until the ruggadization is complete, whether it is unfolding slowly or taking a much longer time than you expected it. God is sieving, straining, churning, picking every characteristic out of you so that you to fit into the manner of His calling. *14th November 2012*

With son, Peter

Teaching beadwork in Nigeria

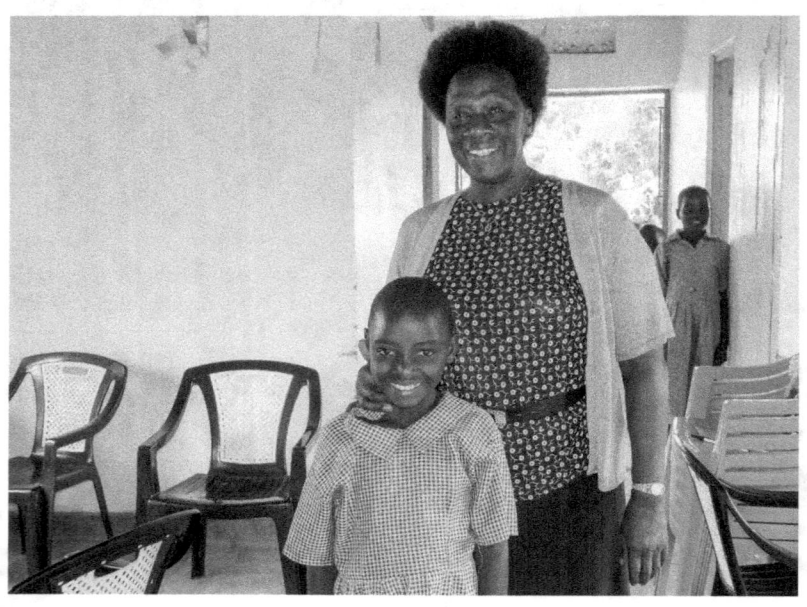

CHAPTER TWO
CON TU AMOR

MERCY AND STEPHIE KEZIE stayed with me for a night. Mercy suggested a Spanish song by Jaci Velasquez and how she knew it and where it was I did not guess. I came back from the kitchen and found it going on. After listening to the song for a long time, I felt so much attached to it even though the words I could not understand but it melted my heart for the Lord because I was sure she was singing about the Lord. So I came with these words:

Only you with your Love, Only you I love
    I did not get married. No one noticed my beauty.
    Those who were about to notice my rare beauty
    You swayed them off, that leave her alone. She is for me.
    Because you saw the rare love in me and wanted to preserve
    It only for yourself. You made me leave all comfortable beds in

The world I have travelled and make me sleep on the floor in order
To grow a tree of love for you my creator.
There is no strong tree or plant that grows
without being planted or grows right from the ground,
so you had to remove me from the hanging bed
and place me on the ground so that I would grow
into a might tree for your divine use.
No wonder most of the loving songs, sermons, devotions, etc.
I have received them on the ground.

Prayer, Lord, what can I say, you chose me, I did not choose you, but found myself just locked in your love, even though at times I find myself in such contradictory corruption and confusion of this world. I find myself on my knees bowing at your feet and crying tears of love. Nothing can stand in between me and your love. Your love Lord cannot be compared with anything in the whole eternity.

Song, Con Tu Amor. Today you have given me one song throughout by Jaci Velasquez: "Con Tu Amor. Only You With Your Love, Only You For Me." I am melting in your love Lord. This love is beyond human understanding only the one who is dwelling in the most high place of Divine can understand it. My parents, my sibling, my friends, my neighbors, my colleagues, my relatives and other people I just knew are all gone but I am still alive hanging only on you, the giver of life. Con Tu

Amor. Emma, Mercy and Kezie are enjoying their sleep. I have failed to sleep, but I know I am in the presence of my maker. I feel no fatigue, no loss of sleep or anything except I am enjoying the presence of the creator of the universe. I feel the whole universe in my heart. I do not know what tomorrow holds for me but I am more than convinced that the Lord of the harvest has the whole world in His hands, He will not leave me nor forsake me. Con Tu Amor. *11th November 2012*

Kasoya doll made by Gertrude Kabatalemwa

New shoes donated from US

CHAPTER THREE
WEDDING OF
PRINCESS OF TOORO

I WOKE up at 5.00am to leave for the village with Emma and we reached Mityana at 7.00am. The van got spoiled so we worked on it up to 11.00 then drove up to Kakungube again when the van got the same problem, The seals had busted and oil was spilling so a mechanic also worked on it. We continued the journey and when we reached Kiganda the van had completely powered all the oil out. Again an old mechanic came and helped us work on it up to 3.00pm and advised us to return to Kampala. On the way back 5 miles to Mityana it broke down again. Within 10 minutes God in His mercy brought a breakdown truck driven by the Angels which had a crane to lift, they lifted the van on the truck and up to Nakawa we went, I got a taxi to home.

Since morning the vehicles were zooming passed us going for the wedding of Princess of Tooro Ruth Komuntale with her American fiancé to take place on 17th November 2012.

When I was still at Mityana I got a great surprise when I bought the news paper of 15th November 2012; that is when there was introduction of Komuntale around her neck there was the necklace I designed myself of the American Flag. There is a message God wants to tell me!!! *16th November 2012*

Ministering in the US

CHAPTER FOUR
BAPTISM OF TRIALS

I WOKE up thanking the Lord for all what He has done.

BAPTISM OF TRIALS, AT HOME ALONE EMMA HAD GONE TO work in the van and Clare come to help me. Emma comes back home to report that gasket cylinder head blew and it will takes another 1.8m/= more, after spending 350,000/=. Then bearings 300,000/= tyres, etc. 400,000/= after I spent 120,000 on repairs and 200,000 crane to tow from Nagulu.

Every trial is designed for a particular individual. God never says, "Oops, made a mistake on that one. I shouldn't have given you that. I meant that for Frank. Sorry, Bob" It's as if the Lord has our name on specific trials. They are specifically designed for us, arranged with our weaknesses and our immaturity in mind. He bears down and doesn't let up.

Each trial is designed after particular individual. You cannot take my trial nor can I take yours thinking how much smaller it is. God has given each person a measure of faith which can carry you through, because each individual has his and her own make of resistance, of shock absorbers or horse power which is designed for each person to keep him going. Some people are short distance runners 100 meters, others run 500 meters and yet others are marathon runners. And we groan and we hurt and we weep and we pray and we grow and we learn. Through it all we learn to depend upon His Word.

Indeed when we get trials, first of all, before we realize the source or origin of the problem we go finger pointing and shifting blames, until we realize that it's a trial from God, then we it down and groan and hurt and weep and pray.

I wept for almost two years when Peter was kidnapped; even I tried suicide but as time went on I got composed and listened to what God was saying. Then I started to pray and God began to speak to me. I learnt how to ask Him questions and how to listen, I learnt how to receive His answers. I learnt how to depend on Him, even when I would meet challenging people, even my own mum would ask me whether I heard properly from God, I had an answer to give quoting what the Lord who told me "It's only me who knows where Peter is, and I am the only one who will bring him back. Peter will return after 20 years."

Chuck Swindoll writes that the common response to trials is Resistance, if not outright Resentment. Whether resistance or resentment, once it has come and it is God ordained you have to wait until when that trial has taken its course, these only women who have given birth will understand. Once the child is due when the labour pains start coming there is no way you can stop them until a child has come out. So the measure or duration God has given the trial has to take its course, months or years, there is no way you can stop it midway.

How much better that we open the doors of our hearts and welcome the God-ordained trials as honored guests for the good they do in our lives writes Chuck Swindoll.

ONE MAY ASK; "WHAT DO YOU MEAN BY GOD ORDAINED TRIALS?"

It is difficult to explain, because trials come in levels. They are those which are short term trials like the one of Esther and Mordecai where Haman wanted to kill him and all the Jews. It took a week or few days when Mordecai came to know it, and within two days Haman was hanged. The middle term trial is the one of Job; all things came boom, boom, then he crawled for 7 years as he went through hell.

And the long term trials are those which takes a long time even a century like the one of Hannah being a barren woman for such a long time and it is mentioned that Peninah, her rival co-wife, used to taunt her year after year when they used to go to offer the sacrifice. For me over thirty years as Peter was missing for 22 years and then Robert was missing for 9 years which that totals up to 31 years. Trials, whether short or long term, they all hurt the same. *17th November 2012*

CHAPTER FIVE
STILL MY HEART IS AT REST

THIS DAY I spent the whole day on the road watching vehicles zooming past us going for the royal wedding while we were stuck on the road. We first got stuck ay Mityana 7.00pm a mechanic arrived and helped us. At Kakungube the Lord brought us a Batooro group, who helped us to reach Kiganda. In Kinganda the Lord got us an old man who worked on the van up to 3.00pm to return to Mityana. After driving 5 miles to Mityana the van completely locked itself when the Lord brought a special crane with an angel who lifted the van at 200,000 ugs up to Nakawa.

All in all, whatever happened my heart was at peace. Whenever something happens the Lord gives me a spirit of serenity and that is what the Lord gave me Emma because for him nothing moves him. Praise the Lord!!! The demographics and strengths, weaknesses, opportunities, and threats (SWOT) of my trials are numerous but the Lord trained me and my children how to bear each other's burdens without blowing our trumpet to let anyone, even the closest friend, know what we are going through. Whenever trials occur we converge to see ways and means how to go into combat so we are shock absorbers for each other. Trials are weighing scales or gages where a true pilgrim Christian is weighed to determine the levels of her or his Christianity. Without going through trials, a Christian is like flesh without bones and flesh without bones cannot stand. *16th November 2012*

WE STARTED AGAIN AT 5.00PM TO GO TO THE VILLAGE AND we reached exactly at the same spot at Kakungube Trading Centre at 7.45am when the van had the same problem. We turned to the same people, the Batooro mechanics. The Lord stopped us at the same spot on Kakungube where we were to get help of the iron bar.

Emma called Kampala and Nicholas responded by midday he had arrived and started removing the hubcap at 3.00pm he finished. As we were winding off to return the tyre Emma was holding the tyre under the van when the jack released, the van came down and landed on the hand of Nicholas with the frame on his back almost breaking his back bone. We were all terrified until Akiiki the older fellow ran and got a big round iron bar and Emma with all his might lifted the van and Nicholas was released. The Lord protected Nicholas so as not to break his hand and the van frame did not to break his back bone. The Lord placed Kagame Mechanic with long experience at Mubende one who knew we were about to arrive totally devastated by the condition of the van. *20th November 2012*

> *Prayer, Thank you, Lord Jesus, you helped us through and through we give you glory. We have seen you at work at every stage it was your hand which shielded and protected us. Blessed Be the name of the Lord. Amen.*

SINCE THE 16TH WHEN THE CLIMAX OF TROUBLES PEAKED I had suspended sleep. My prayers have been deep, interceding, and spiritual prayers carefully selected. I have been so sad of all what has been happening to me, there has been a growing climax of spiritual events where the enemy has doubled, even tripled whatever he has ever done before with acts of rebellion enough to make me mad to the extent of losing my head where I start Fighting the wind! But the Lord has given me the spirit of serenity in such a time of these storms, hurricanes, tornadoes, cyclones, earthquakes, and hailstones.

2012 Trials

- January - Girl runs away from home.
- February - Van breaks down with Louisiana Team at Rwibale.
- March - Visitor comes from USA and starts behaving wildly and then returns.
- April – In Kihooza a tree fell on the latrine and people came to invade the home.
- May - Worker's behavior changed when teaming with workers.
- June - Amber House battle goes on since June to date.
- July - Teacher caught student stealing bananas and left.
- July - Another one runs away and this reveals all the evil they were doing.
- August to October - Visiting women from another town were drinking, stealing, and doing witchcraft.
- September - Tractor came crashing into the house.

- September to November - Nyamabuga hailstone storms damaged only the school 3 times.
- October - Bunga House, water and electricity bills were in the extreme.
- November - Van episodes between Kampala and village from 16th - 24th.
- December 24th - My phone was stolen from the container which brought much commotion within the community.

> *Prayer, Lord, I am at the climax of all the calamities the enemy has brought to crash me down, but you Lord, have seen me through all this and I am grateful. This morning I am asking: is this the time Lord? Are you to relieve me out of this world and crown me with the crown of victory in death? Or will You bless me with life in this world to show the world your glory? Amen.*

I RESISTED OPENING MY EMAIL BOX UNTIL I FINISHED pouring my heart to the Lord. As soon as I finished powering my heart to God, after I opened my email box there an email from a bother was waiting for me:

Date: November 20, 2012 5:22:30 PM CST To: Sister Gertrude

Sister G, I am finally back on my home time schedule. It was good to visit with you in Kampala. I am writing to say that I am forwarding a gift for your ministry in the amount of $20,000. I will send this gift to Neepuganda in California next week. I hope this is an encouragement to you. The donor wants the gift used where needed most. I will provide a tax-deductible receipt for this donor. Greet Emma and Claire. Everyone sends their greetings. We will be returning to Uganda in March to teach the 11-15th in Kampala After this email I started powering tears of thanksgiving.

> *Prayer, Lord, let these tears run to your Throne Room like Pearls!!! Lord, let these tears run to you in your Throne Room in the colors of a rainbow!!! Lord, let these tears run to you in your Throne Room as the river of pure gold!!! Amen.*

LEFT WITH KARWANI FOR TOWN TO TAKE THE VEHICLE'S repair. They removed the gear box to identify the problem of the 4wheel drive memory box and found the sensors had locked.

We had to leave the van in the garage so I hired the Taxi and came back. *Still my heart is at rest.* I spent the night at school. 21st November 2012

CHAPTER SIX
GOD'S SAINTS ARE NOT INSTANTLY MADE

I SPENT the night at school with no sleep. In a vision I saw a very ugly, defeated, and scared dog running away with its tail tucked in between its legs. In the spirit that was my enemy. *22nd November 2012*

BY OPENING THE BIBLE THE LORD GAVE ME A MESSAGE THAT Paul did not preach because it was not yet written, but he ministered by teaching people in Roman, Corinthian, etc. I went to minister in the church on the above messages. *25th November 2012*

ALL THE DAY I WAS WORKING IN THE COMPOUND.
Message, God's Saints are not Instantly made, each one is Hand-Tooled, by the Maker according to His Choice and Call-

ing. The present age we are living in the people, whether Christians or not Christians, are instinctively doing things in such a hurry like there is no tomorrow. They see the time is spinning away. In actual sense time was running at super speed before the hurricane Sandy Storm which hit New York.

The Lord showed it to me in a dream. I was standing outside and watching towards the sky and there seemed to be nobody in the world. In the sky clouds started passing at such speed but then unfolded before me after passing, some with messages, others with maps. I saw one country unfolding before me and another, I heard its name and the word was Judgment. After one weekend. The storm Sandy, a super storm, hit New York. Things were happening so fast. That's the way life is today, Fast, Compressed, Condensed and Slam-bang-it's-done. Not so in God's wilderness schooling, when it comes to walking with God there is no such thing as instant maturity. God doesn't mass produce His saints He hand *tools each one and* it always takes a lot longer than we expect. *28th November* 2012

I WAS FEELING SO MUCH OF LOVE FOR THE LORD. HE SPOKE to me, that He is the one who performs great things, the impossibilities, and the imaginable. He makes kings out of the shepherds. He makes rulers out of the slaves. He makes queens out of captives. He makes great administrators out of exiles. He makes barren women mothers. He brings *back the captiv*e tha**t** was kidnapped. He brings back home the runaways. *2nd December 2012*

I found out that when Peter came home and used my iPad he touched a wrong key on my emails so I could not open my emails and he created a twitter account for himself.

Termite Syndrome, I woke up with a prayer for Uganda, this time I was not emotional but prayed composed putting fact by fact to God, until I came to a corruption termite syndrome. From 1962 - 1971 Milton Obote was possessed by Common Man's Chatter which was driving Ugandans to slavery of communism and socialism. God helped Uganda.

Also, Ugandans had completely forgotten God but God remembered us and used Idi Amin who with a gun he took over the power from Obote who had gone to Singapore to attend a conference. Amin started killing whole tribes because he did not like educated people and he thought would over throw his power.

Amin gave 90 days for Indians to leave Uganda soil and gave their businesses to his fellow Nubians and Moslems. All nations sanctioned Uganda to punish Amin so Uganda could not trade with any country. We went into a crisis of economic war where shops were stocked with ripe bananas and pan cakes. In order for God to sustain Uganda He gave Uganda a coffee boom and caused frost to fall on Brazil's coffee plantations.

Before Brazil was the leading coffee producer in the world but their coffee dried up. Amin banned all other Christian groups whom he knew that could invoke God and some were imprisoned and others like Catholics, Protestants and Moslems left. Then most of the Christians went into underground churches and prayed and God heard. On 27th June 1976 Idi Amin allowed the terrorists who hijacked Air France Airbus Flight No. 139 to land at Entebbe Airport.

The terrorists wanted to cause the release of 53 convicted fellow terrorists held in Israel, and this paralyzed the whole world. God caused Amin to go and invade Tanzania and

Tanzania in retaliation came up to Uganda and drove Amin out of Uganda in April 1979. Ugandans celebrated not knowing what was coming. After the Tanzanians went back many leaders came and started Fighting for power eventually so Obote emerged from 1980.

Again, the rule of murder and terror started. There was Panda Gali and most of our young men were killed in the name of looking for the rebels. On 27th July 1985 Obote was run out of Uganda to Kenya then to Zambia. Uganda was in Turmoil. Okello Lutwa and Bazillio Okello were illiterate presidents who took over the government and started Peace Talks with the Rebels led by Yoweri Museveni.

On 26th January 1986 Museveni arrived in Kampala and took power. He was straight about swearing to finish corruption, a with forgiveness attitude, quoting the Bible all the time, promising to put things right and quit condemning African presidents who had taken on presidency till death. Year after year he started to bring in in-laws like son and wife. Uganda became like a family business. The abrogation of the constitution in 1994 caused people to start doubting our president Museveni. The termites of corruption in Uganda started eating up departments with companies becoming parastatal bodies, ministries, parliament, State House and now the Prime Minister's Office. An ant hill of corruption had built up in Uganda and the ants have eaten up all the foundation from the poles to the top. Only our God is going *to flush out a*nd remove the queen ant and all the termites will disperse. *3rd December* 2012

WHEN THE DEVIL THINKS THAT HE HAS PUT ME TO SLEEP and he pours cold water in my kettle and puts-on the lid the Holy

Spirit starts warming me up. Next the devil sees I am getting hot, then I start to bubble, the siren goes, the lid is lifted and the steam of my prayers go up and I have escaped from the devil's snare. The sun, moon and stars are the scaffolds and frame work out works of that glorious building where the blessed inhabit, that house not made with hands. No way to Heaven but by Jesus Christ.

Without a personal relationship with Jesus Christ your life is a mockery, fake. It's *counterfeit. 6th December 2012*

MUSEVENI WAS REPORTED THAT HE HAD GONE TO VISIT Putin in Russia, this was after 12 European donor countries stopped their support to Uganda because of mass corruption in OPM's office. The Bible tells a similar way where the Lord said: the king who trusted Egypt, that it was like leaning on a reed which will break and jab your hand, so is Pharaoh of Egypt if you trust him. Isaiah 36:6.

I was very sick again with nausea, headache, and stomach ache. I took malaria tabs but was getting worse and at 3.00 pm ran to Rhona Clinic where they checked my whole blood and found typhoid. Already my sight has gone bad, joints *ached, appetite l*ost, skin had turned dark, stiff joints *and my body was feeling* heavy. *10th December 2012*

I AM STILL ON TREATMENT AT HOME. *11TH DECEMBER 2012*

I LEFT KAMPALA WITH EMMA AT 11.00AM FOR THE VILLAGE and arrived at 4.00pm. Rumours from false prophets said it was the *day to be the en*d of the world and I waited for it until midnight but it never came to pass. *12th December* 2012

CHAPTER SEVEN
YOU DO NOT KNOW ME

YOU DO NOT KNOW ME, No one can understand a spirit filled person in this world. If you want to understand a spirit filled person you need to get in the spirit too. But if you do not you will never understand him. Even when people try to do research on you they will be disappointed because where they expect to find you, they will not find you there.

People expect you to think, talk and walk the same way they do things, but the spiritual person has a different way of thinking, talking and walking, because of being led by the spirit. A spiritual person is not loved at all, even among his own, because always he speaks the truth and the world does not want the truth.

Prophet Jeremiah was called a weeping prophet because always he spoke of the truth to the kings and gave warnings to the children of Israel. And he was much hated to the extent of almost being put to death several times. When the worldly people and fellow Christians speak well of you, you know that you are swimming in the same waters and there is no difference between you and them. When you speak judgment and warning to these people they will hate you with all their passion.

In the Old Testament major prophets were not loved because

of the warnings and judgments they prophesied against the land, kings and people of Israel. Ezekiel had to make a judgment against the nations, Ezekiel 25:1-32. Elijah had to run for his life from Jezebel, 1 Kings 19:2-8. Isaiah was sent by God to tell the judgment against the nation, Isaiah 13:1-23 and 23:18. Jeremiah had to hide and was imprisoned after twice writing about God's anger and coming wrath for Judah, Jeremiah 36 to 38; and Daniel kept matters in his heart in Daniel 6 and 7.

People will expect you to have the certain size of a house and a car that changes as the world changes. You have to have a big stomach like other big men, speak the language of rich men, women will have to turn your hair blue or purple, wear extensions on your fingernails or even put on trousers, etc. If you do not do these things, the worldly people will be disappointed. They want you to change your appearance so they have something to talk about even though they are not the ones enjoying these things.

However, whether you do them or ignore them it does not stop them talking, because at least they want to catch you on the wrong foot and have something to talk about.

Everything about you hurts them. When they are going to a wrong church, knowing or not knowing, they want you to be their too so that their conscious does not condemn them and so that they are not in it alone but all going the same road. When they see that you have created a gap that they cannot close, they will send an emissary or agent who will come to fish out information to know what is happening around you.

They want to know where do you get your strength, your finance break through, who are your friends because you no longer go to tell them your problems or ask for assistance which they did not give you even when you needed it. At least they want to know where you stand. When you keep your distance they are sad because they do not want to lose track of you so they will send a Christian or relative to come as an advisor or sympathizer, e.g. Sam and Robert experience.

People always want you to be with them even when they know that you are all going nowhere, they are happy because you are comrades; but once they know you have cut a corner and are breaking away from their hook they do not like it because they do not want you go away and leave them. If they realize that you have broken away, they will start to create stories to damage or tarnish your name and to draw away people who would come close to you.

They will call you names, e.g. crazy, Jesus freak, very bad, etc. When they see you are still not bothered by those statements they will create something more hurting, e.g. drug dealers, terrorist that cuts heads off people, satanists, witch, murderer, child defiler, etc. But all this is to appease their conscious. When you went through situations no one cared or said let's go and help and they only talked and made your suffering because of gossip among themselves; they would say this time she or he is finished. You do not know me!!! Whether you are my blood sister or brother if you are not in the spirit we are two different people.

When God is after you He will separate you from everybody who does not benefit you for His purpose. Why should you hang around people who talk sweet nothings? Talk about TV programs with episodes of men and women, who is befriending who, who killed who, who is dating who, they discuss football teams even Christian Pastors are supporting football teams and radio stations are even giving it air times while the People of God are perishing from not hearing about Jesus.

Angelica Zambrano of Equador said when she was dead for 23 hours and she was in heaven when she saw our Lord crying. When she inquired why He was crying He said many of my people are going to hell and few are coming to heaven. She saw people dropping in hell as grains of sand.

You do not know me!!! If you are a committed Christian, You will be my friend as long as you continue doing the right things before God and you do not need to try pleasing me or seeking favor from me. I am also a human being, so as long as you please God when I see you, I see a "Yes" on you, I feel the peace in my heart and I know you are accepted before the Lord and who am I to say "No?" You do not need to tell me that you have been repenting.

Every time you start doing things which distance you from God, people who are close to the Holy Spirit will feel it. Some of their hearts get stirred in anger and they see you ugly and you dismiss yourself without being sent away. So, when you notice that the only thing to do is go and make peace with God and immediately the cloud or rejection is lifted and peace of the Lord returns.

You do not know me!!! You do not know a spiritual man because you do not know his relationship with his Creator. You see a spiritual man during the day but do not know how they spends their private time; while your time is spent in bars, casinos, or gossiping about football teams or episodes on TV, e.g. soap operas, the man of God spends time seeking God. By the time He wakes up all his debts are paid and the capital is deposited in the bank because the favor and anointing of the *Lord is upon him.* Whatever is got from God is clean and has no strings attached. You do not know me!!! 13th December 2012

I WORKED *SO HARD AT THE FARM* IN THE POTATO GARDEN AND came back so tired that I did not even pray. I went to bed. *15th December* 2012

ON EARLY IN THE MORNING IT STARTED RAINING SO HARD I could hear the sky rumbling full of anger and the rain was just pouring. I pulled my blanket so I could sleep some more, early morning rain is my favorite time where I enjoy sleep. But I heard a Still Small Voice saying Baitu Toimuka? I jerked out of bed, and started praying then the sky and rain subsided.

Prayer, *as wicked people* live doing evil unconsciously let me always live unconsciously doing righteously good. Amen. *16th December 2012*

I WOKE UP AND PRAYED FOR SOULS IN MINDANAO AND NEW YORK where Super Sandy storm hit. On 9th December 2012 before Super Sandy Storm hit New York, Mindanao was hit by typhoon and earth*quake which was a*gain th**e** Judgment I saw for Asia. In Mindanao 548 people died and thousands were left homeless. *17th December 2012*

CHAPTER EIGHT
DISCOVERY, LIFE OF YOURSELF, SERENDIPITY

I WOKE up simply thinking not much of anything but opened my email and re-read Charles Swindoll's message: The Beauty of God's Holiness.

> *Message, Holy, holy, holy is the Lord God, the Almighty, who was and who is and who is to come. Revelation 4:8.*

There is many a time I have woken up asking myself; what life is all about? Is it eating, drinking, going out to work only to come back home continuously without breaking that monotony? This day I found an answer to this long-time question from Bro Chuck Swindoll's Insight, that serendipity is a happy luck find that takes the form of finding valuable thing that are not looked for a serendipitous discovery.

However, in this life we need to break that monotonous life by finding divine valuables or things that are always not locked for. We need to live a discovery life in God. And this discovery life occurs when something beautiful breaks from the monotony of a dull and ordinary mundane life of eating, drinking, sleeping, then waking up and going to work.

At times I pity house wives, their lives are monotonous waking up, cleaning, going to look for food, cooking, etc. life goes on like that day in day out. You may say that you do not live a monotonous life because you break it with watching the TV or going to support your football team, you go to a bar or a night club, you go to a casino, you go to drinking parties and you say this gives you excitement. But how long does this excitement last? And do they promise you a peaceful end?

Our Lord took Bernarda Fernandez to heaven and hell and when she was in hell she asked the Lord if there was somebody she knew in hell. The Lord brought her Alexandre and in her own words she said: I turned toward the Lord and asked Him: "Is there anyone from my family in this hell?" He answered me "I will not allow you to see a member of your family." I asked Him again: "Lord is there anyone that I know here?" "Yes", said the Lord and I will allow you to see him. Suddenly I saw a young man coming from the depths of the hell: It was Alexandre.

I knew this young man at a crusade my husband I attended in Dominica Republic. During that crusade, I heard a voice saying to me, "Get up, go and meet Alexandre who is passing by. Tell him not to reject this message, for I'm giving him a last chance." This voice was the voice of the Lord even though I did not see Him. I told Alexandre what the Lord told me.

This is how he responded: "You Christians are all fools. You deceive people by telling them that Jesus Christ is coming, I, Alexandre, do not believe this to be the truth." I told him: "Alexandre, God gives live and takes it away when he wants; Alexandre, you will soon die." He answered: "I am too young to die, I still have many good years of festivities on this earth." This chance was well and truly the last for Alexandre. Dear reader, what do you know about yourself? Three weeks later,

Alexandre died while he was drunk. His destination was this place of torment where I saw him (hell). The Bible states clearly that drunkard will not inherit the kingdom of God. Galatians 5:21.

When looking at people in hell, I could see Alexandre attacked by two big worms. He was screaming "Ouch! Ouch! Ouch!" He was tormented. He recognized me and told me: "I neglected my last chance. I am here today, suffering. Please, when you return to earth, go to my house and tell my family to believe in Jesus Christ and to obey His word, so that they will not come to this place of torment." Then she asked Him again: "Are there Christians in this hell?" He answered: "Yes, do you know why? They believed in Me but they did not walk according to my Word."

THERE ARE MANY, THOSE CHRISTIANS WHO ONLY BEHAVE WELL, WHEN THEY ARE IN THE CHURCH

There are many, those Christians who only behave well, when they are in the Church, in front of their pastors and their family. But they are greatly deceiving themselves. The eyes of my Father see everything and He understands every word, wherever you are. Tell my people that it's time they lived a holy life before my Father, before the devil and before the world. Let the devil has no right to accuse my people; and let the world not pointing finger at my people. It's high time we sought holiness and consecration, 1 Peter 1:14-16; by Bernarda Fernandez.

At that moment I saw Jesus weeping and He told me again that there are too many of those who are lost, more than those who go to heaven. Then Jesus showed me the number of people who were dying in a minute and He told me: Look! How many are lost! My Church is sleeping despite the fact that she has received my power. She has my word and the Holy Spirit but She is sleeping. On earth there are people who preach that Hell does not exist. Go and tell them that this place is real.

We need something different and something exciting which will lead us to eternal life. Accept Jesus Christ as your Lord and saviour and you will break a monotonous dull life and He will give you a life which you are thinking is exciting. You are in the midst of death. Start now for an exciting life of great expectancy with ability of ending your life peacefully. This much I know, the Lord delights in surprising us. He dots our pilgrimage from earth to heaven with amazing serendipities with discoveries, e.g.

Praise and Worship, close relationship, meaningful dreams, visions, and revelation, having others for sharing experiences, etc. All day and night you will see you are living in miracles. At this moment you may find your life is so useless and at times you ask yourself why Am I living? Some of you have tried to take your life away, I did it many times before I met the Lord. My life was meaningless and I was tired, yet I was only in my 20s. Until when I came to know the Lord in my 30s then Life became meaningful with excitement and since then, from now on I am always on the lookout for the time when the Lord calls me home. Therefore you also, be on the lookout; God may very well be planning for you to start a life of discovering yourself in divine excitement as you wait for His return.

"Serendipity occurs when something beautiful breaks into the monotonous and the mundane. A serendipitous life is marked by surprise and spontaneity. When we lose our capacity for either, we settle into life's ruts. We expect little and we're seldom disappointed. Though I have walked with God for several decades, I must confess I still find much about Him incomprehensible and mysterious. But this much I know: He delights in surprising us. He dots our pilgrimage from earth to heaven with amazing serendipity. Your situation may be as hot and barren as a desert or as forlorn and meaningless as a wasteland, but all I ask is that you be on the lookout.

God may very well be plan*ning serendipity fo*r your life." (Chuck Swindoll)

Clare, Mercy and Stephanie arrived with Link Bus and I met them at Rugombe. *18th December 2012*

EMMA AND JOHN ARRIVED WITH SIGN POST MATERIALS AS WE worked on the whole day. *21st December 2012*

CHAPTER NINE
TWO DREAMS

DREAM, a big building, amber in colour, was standing among the dilapidated buildings with bare bricks, other building was crumpling. The building was shaped with different towers, high and low. Influential people of the town came to ask me when I purchased the land to put such a building. Also, I was wondering but later I asked them how could I put up such a building up without first buying the land? I was assured that I had the land title for that land.

This is in reference of what the Lord told me that He has the Title Deed for Amber House.

I sold my prize bull at 1,200,000. *Clare and I went to* visit Richard Bangirana and Loy at Kyarusozi and had so many things to pray about when we returned home at 10.00pm. *23rd December 2012*

ALL OF US AT THE SCHOOL WERE WORKING ON THE SCHOOL in the front compound and then returned home at 11.00pm. My phone disappeared in *the bag, my knee w*as floating in fluid but I was rejoicing in the Lord, I was not afraid because the Lord is going to heal me as usual. *24th December 2012*

DREAM, AT 8.00AM KAMPALA WAS IN DARKNESS. I WAS TOLD by Peter that there were bombs planted in tall buildings. There were no vehicles on the streets only police; 999 is the one which picked me and Clare to t*ake us home. We pr*ayed at Kyarusozi church for the situation. *30th December 2012*

I WAS WORKING AT THE SCHOOL COMPOUND TILL LATE IN the evening, then prepared supper for all of us and lit the fire for me, Kangume and Monday. We prayed and worshipped the Lord till 2.00am on 1st Jan 2013. *31st December 2012*

END OF 2012

CHAPTER TEN
CHANGE A "NO" FACE TO A
"YES" FACE

BEGINNING of 2013

I WAS WORKING IN THE COMPOUND WHEN PASTOR Kanyalyoya came to see me and we shared. There are four witnesses who do not lie and cannot be bribed. One, is your Heart's conviction, two is the soil where you stand to commit an act, three is the heavens which watch you doing the act, and four is God who sees everything we do. *2nd January 2013*

CANDIDLY, I KNOW OF NOTHING THAT HAS THE POWER TO change us from within like the freedom that comes through grace. It's so amazing it will change not only our hearts but also our faces. And goodness knows, some of us are overdue for a face change! Were you reared by parents whose faces said "No?" Or are you married to someone with a "No" face? If that is true, you envy those who had "Yes" face parents or are married to "Yes" face mates.

All of us are drawn to those whose faces invite us in and urge us on. During his days as president Thomas Jefferson and a group of companions were traveling across the country on horseback. They came to a river which had left its banks because of a recent downpour. The swollen river had washed the bridge away. Each rider was forced to ford the river on horseback, Fighting for his life against the rapid currents.

The very real possibility of death threatened each rider, which caused a traveler who was not part of their group to step aside and watch. After several had plunged in and made it to the other side, the stranger asked President Jefferson if he would ferry him across the river. The president agreed without hesitation. The man climbed on, and shortly there after the two of them made it safely to the other side.

As the stranger slid off the back of the saddle onto dry ground, one in the group asked him, "Tell me, why did you select the president to ask this favor of?" The man was shocked, admitting he had no idea it was the president who had helped him. "All I know," he said, "is that on some of your faces was written the answer 'No' and on some of them was the answer 'Yes;' His was a 'Yes' face."

Freedom gives people a "Yes" face. I am confident Jesus had a "Yes" face. I have never seen Him, but I've determined from w hat I've read about Him that this was true. What a contrast He must have been! He was surrounded by lettered men, religious, robed, righteous, law-quoting, professional men whose very demeanor announced "No!" Pious without, killers within . . . yet none of their poison seeped into His life. On the contrary, He revolutionized the entire direction of religion because He announced "Yes" while all His professional peers were frowning "No." That has intrigued me for years. How could it be?

What was it that kept Him from getting caught in their grip? In one word, it was grace. He was so full of truth and grace, He left no inner space for their legalistic poison. My prayer, Lord, as I continue on Your mission, may you let people see The answer "Yes or a Right" on me, but only to people You have destined or directed to walk with me. Also, please let me see a "Yes or Right" on people as You send me on this mission. Which face do you wear? Some people are born with "accepted" faces marked "Yes or Right" on their face but other people are born with "rejected" faces marked "No." But there are those who Work Hard to change a "No" face to a "Yes" face. *3rd January 2013*

CHAPTER ELEVEN
MY OTHER NAME IS KABATALEMWA TIGALYOMA

SONG, I woke up with the song "Jesus You Are So Good" by Don Moen.

WHERE HE SAYS YOU GIVE ME CONFIDENCE, YOU ARE MY provider, I just want to thank you with everything of my heart. On this point I remembered how The Lord has been providing for me, and others using me for feeding families and individuals since 1996.

In 1996 to date I have helped women, widows and orphans giving them work through the Crafts Projects, from 1997 to date there have been men and women who have been helped through Amber House Programmes, and since 2001 to date I have been working with men, women, and families through Nyamabuga School Projects.

On these points I considered how He has provided for me throughout the years even though I do not get a salary but I have never lacked. He provides food, shelter, security on the road when I travel back and forth from Kampala to the village, every time I am under His wings. I saw how He has been providing towards the School Building since 2001, step-by-step to the stage where the building is now. And this has made me shed many tears, where Amber House Ltd. Management wanted to throw me out by increasing rent month by month.

This time when it reached a climax and they wanted me to pay 54m/= and He paid it miraculously through a secret donor who did not want his name to be mentioned... Thank you Brother D.

At this point I cried so much and I suggested another name to be added to Kabatalemwa.

First in 2012 added was Hakiire Kabatalemwa, and then on 5th January 2013 added was Tigalyoma Kabatalemwa.

Hakiire, meaning that even if everyone will disappoint you Lord, but when you look at me, always find me doing the right thing. When anyone makes you cry Lord, when You look at me, **Smile and say at** least Kabatalemwa always cheers My Heart.

Tigalyoma, meaning the tears of my thanksgiving will never dry after I got a message that Robert has arrived. *5th January 2013*

MY PLEA IS THAT WE DO NOT LIMIT GRACE TO CHRIST. WE, too, can learn to be just as gracious as He. And since we can, we must not only show grace in our words and in great acts of compassion and understanding but in small ways as well. Let me describe four practical expectations you can anticipate as you get a firm grasp on grace. First, you can expect to gain a greater appreciation for God's gifts to you and others.

What gifts? Several come to mind. The free gift of salvation. The gift of life. The gift of laughter, music, beauty, friendship, and forgiveness. Those who claim the freedom God offers gain an appreciation for the gifts that come with life. Second, you can expect to spend less time and energy being critical of and concerned about others' choices. Wouldn't that be a refreshing relief? When you get a grasp on grace you begin to operate in a context of freedom and you become increasingly less petty.

You will allow others room to make their own decisions in life, even though you may choose otherwise. Third, you can expect to become more tolerant and less judgmental. Externals will not mean as much to you. You'll begin to cultivate a desire for authentic faith rather than endure a religion based on superficial performance. You will find yourself so involved in your own pursuit of grace, you'll no longer lay guilt trips on those with whom you disagree. Fourth, you can expect to take a giant step toward maturity.

As your world expands, thanks to an awakening of your understanding of grace, your maturity will enlarge. Before your very eyes, new vistas will open. It will be so transforming, you will never be the same. *7th January 2013*

ALL DAY I WAS SO BUSY WITH THE SCHOOL CHORES. IN THE evening I went to visit Richard Mugabyomu and take him something for the preparation of his daughter's introduction. So, I kept thinking that is the little girl I saw hanging on the side of her father, now she has finished the university, got a good job and now is getting married. Not only that, now she is having so much money to sponsor the refurbishing her father's house. God has designed each person's life and we should not do comparisons with anybody.

You are you and I am myself with different set ups. So, I woke up in such wonder, seeing my precious daughter and son Working with me without a salary but content and standing with me in all my Trials. The Lord who blesses His people at the Prime of their Lives is the same Lord who blesses others in their late advanced lives.

Immediately, I saw my Great Manifestation of the Little Insect, tinier than a period, full stop, moving on the face of my iPad. I followed it across and I started worshiping the Lord, How He cares and remembered me when He told me to see Him in His creation. My Father, my God, my Lord and my Creator always my heart will Honour You. So, when before my very eyes, God opens new vistas to show me the Works of His hands, so transforming, they leave me completely changed. *8th January 2013*

I WOKE UP AT 1.12AM WITH A QUESTION OF MY LIFE AND MY family how God has kept me behind the curtains without any excitement but just working and trusting Him all the time.

> *Prayer, I started airing a simple prayer to my Lord, Lord it's only You who know what is happening in my life, it's You who made me and it's You who knows the future of my family. Amen.*

CHAPTER TWELVE
KEEP LOVING GOD, HE WILL LIVE

I LEARNED of Solomon's wealth and power, e.g. where he had 4,000 stalls for horses and chariots and 12,000 horsemen which meant each stall had 3 horsemen who were in charge. All Kings of the earth sought the presence of Solomon's wisdom which God had put in his heart. Solomon's son Rehoboam was not wise like his father, he was seeking advise and in doing so he rejected the good advise of elders and took the wrong advise of the youth and messed up Israel and it broke into two kingdoms. So, the king *did not listen to* the people, for it was a turn of events from God, that the Lord might establish His Word, which He spoke through Ahijah. Solomon's love turned to women, 2 Chron. 9 and 10. 10th January 2013

I WOKE UP DISTURBED AND I READ THE WORD, THE HOLY Spirit led me to read, May the Lord answer you and grant all your requests in Psalms 20; Then praise for all the blessings God gave king David in Psalm 21 as a prayer for me. In Psalm 22 is about the Lord's suffering on the cross revealed to king David. These psalms soothed my spirit as I was so perturbed about the situation of my enemies. Clare insisted that I had to see the doctor concerning my swollen legs and I went for blood test.

In October I declared that the Lord was going to pay my debt, and the Lord did as I spoke, He gave me 20,000 to pay the debt. After my blood test as I was coming down rejoicing, I met Bro Mayanja, he was so happy to see me he reached in his pocket and pulled 50,000 and gave it to me as a gesture of welcoming me in the New Year!!! This seed the Lord will multiply 50,000 x 100 times, this very year for His work for Amber House and Nyamabuga building projects. In April someone sent me $50,000 to work on the underground tank.

> *Prayer, Lord, help me as long as I live, let me never trust, anybody to recommend or stand surety. Amen.* 15th January 2013

Pastor Serwadda's sermon, Genesis 26. It does not matter how you start but how you end. Your door of success may be hidden in somebody else, e.g. Laban and Jacob, or Potiphar and Joseph, or Haman and Mordecai. Isaac had no peace in Gerar where the Lord told him to settle and even though his father Abraham's wells were still there this did not stop the people of Gerar from being jealous of him. This was so because he prospered more than them. Even Abimelech the king himself said, "Go away from us for you are too powerful for us."

When you are still the same with the community, speaking the same language, you are on the same level and no one hates you because you are still going to the same well, same market, and sitting in the same bar, and sharing the same jokes, everyone will say you are one of us; but when you take a step further from them they will disown you and become jealous of you because you are getting a head of them, they cannot understand you. What you are doing becomes heavy for them, that's why they will say go away from us. Leave us alone. Even your own close friends and relatives will disown you.

They will call you names like you have wise acre!!! They will look for something to furnish your name to sacrifice people, you may go underwater, etc. But God will combine all their wisdom and give it to you and you will continue excelling. Whatever you are doing it hurts them (Kibaluma) even when it is to benefit them. Because even if the water they are drinking is in your land or their cows graze on your farm they will speak evil about you. Your name becomes a household name, no one can sleep without saying your name. Even when children who are suckling begin to talk, they talk about your name.

Because you are above them, you make their heart throb. A competitor cannot beat you because he uses a lot of strength and hatred to Fight you when you have no time to think about him, instead you are getting more wisdom to get a head of him. Message, Rehoboth, Isaac's well, God has expanded us and we will be fruitful. Isaac built an altar, he built a tent, and he dug a well, Genesis 26:25.

IT DOES NOT MATTER HOW YOU START BUT HOW YOU END.

At 11.31pm a powerful radio station at Nyamabuga began to declare the kingdom of God. God used me to take His Good News to kings and leaders of the world. God opened all their doors of blessings for Clare and Emma to serve with me. God took over Amber House for His Glory and constructed God's Grace Towers.

Robert's return fulfills my God's Testimony. Family returns to Prince Charles Drive Plot No. 6. God's promises for Peter to preach the Gospel of the Kingdom. Nyamabuga Foundation

School Campus has been constructed and is complete. The expansion of Harwera farm to feed nations is done. A village house, helicopter, and personal jet. *20th January 2013*

Pastor Rwere's Teaching, the church of Christ of today's teaching is stirring greed, not the Love of God. One comes out of church bubbling with greed, how to get this, how to get that and where to get it, Not saying I think I need to seek God more or how can I get close to God. Who is burning to seek intimation with his Creator.

He again said there is a Revolution coming in the Pentecostal Church as the Lord showed it to me on 21st July 2012. Apostasy. Breaking away. Combination of Great Break Away. This Combination of Break Away is going to be the last, which is going to see our Lord's Return, no more time. He has said it over and over again that He is Coming again, sooner than expected."

He also talked of altars, individual altars, family altars, area altars, kingdom altars, and territorial altars. All these can affect a nation's politics, societies and economy. Our God hates the idolatry and witchcraft which have dominated this land. Idolatry and witchcraft have erected altars driving the altars of God out, e.g. people who used to call Christians to dedicate and pray when erecting schools now they call witchdoctors. *21st January 2013*

HOLY SPIRIT TO HUMAN SPIRIT CONVERSATION IS THE wisdom God gives, it is not like the one the world gives. The one God gives is Simple and Full of insight. It could tell you to watch and study the little insect, so tiny more than a full stop, moving across the Bible Pages. It walks, it jumps, and it flies. The Lord tells you if you want to know Me or to see Me, first look at that tiny insect and the work of My hands. Again, observe every blade of the grass and that is where you will see Me. I talk through every creation.

My name is the Creator. I lead the people I love in simplicity. In lowly that is where my strength is. You may consider yourself not doing great duty to the Lord, if you are not on the radio, TV or having congregation to cheer you up, but there is a way God uses you in a still quiet way, slowly but a big surely. It is like a barkcloth burning, the fire burns under without alerting anybody until the barkcloth is consumed.

Simple lowly life of a true Christian is not noticed by many but only those God has given insight. You live in an island or isolated life, but the fire of God keeps burning and consuming all the undesired characters in you, e.g. pride, greed, haughtiness, and self. At times you may think to blame yourself that you are not making any steps, while others are racing in a marathon.

But when you are a chosen vessel and the Marathon is inside you will be seen and conducted by your Creator as a D-Day, decision day. Consider our Lord for 3 years He was teaching, preaching, healing and raising the dead. Only a few noticed Him, the fire was kept inside even on the day He was arrested. He did not reveal who He was even when Pilate asked Him questions like "Are you the King of the Jews?" He said, "you have said so." Up to the final hour when He committed His Soul to His Father and said, "It is Finished."

The soul which seeks God will not die. It is a deep, deep well where you draw and draw, and it does not get dry. The water from that well quenches the thirsty. One Word, Jesus, carries so much more meaning than a complete sermon of 2 hours because one Word from God is like a flash that will give you a whole story.

This morning in a flash I saw respected ladies putting on very expensive gowns sitting against big white pillars with their legs stretched out speaking in low tones as those do who have lost a very important person. I heard in my spirit that when this big person dies it will cause me to open doors for my people to enter to that place.

Some people who shout and howl are like bush fires which are seen quickly, and everyone is concerned, and the enemy quickly looks for ways and means to quench the fire, or he lets you continue shouting. The enemy has tricks to drives you further and further from the truth and you remain with the praise and cheers of people carrying chairs in the air throwing money at you because you have stirred their hearts into prosperity gospel. When you say the first person who runs here with a million shillings, it will be multiplied 100 times; or everyone who comes to such and such place will go back with a vehicle, plot, wife, husband, etc. you have been carried away and have misled the people of God. *22nd January* 2013

I AM IN THE GARDEN WITH CHILDREN AND FARMS BOYS removing husks and collecting heaps of maize from the garden. 29th January 2013

IT HAS BEEN ONE WEEK AND I HAVE CONTINUED TO REMOVE the maize husks, now alone in the big garden. I was in d*eep prayer and aske*d The Lord to visit me like Gideon, Manoah's wife, Elizabeth and Mother Mary. He answered me saying I will do something to let you know that I was here with you even if I do not appear physically. 4th February 2013

I SPENT THE DAY AT HOME RESTING. CLARE AND MERCY came and we stayed together.

Message, when I was praying for a young man I got this message: "Let him keep Loving God, He will live." This was a strong statement. If we keep loving God there is nothing that can come between us because the love of God keeps us undercover. Whatever the devil tries in the heavenlies, on ground, underground, on water and underwater to bring against us will not succeed. Amen. Before I went to sleep, I was listening on the Prime Radio to a preacher was teaching about the Sabbath.

I kept wondering and asking myself questions about how that the enemy has duped many. The Seventh Adventists he gave them to keep the sabbath and deny the Great Salvation. Pentecostals got great salvation and hide from them on the sabbath.

Keeping the Sabbath is one of the Ten Commandments, the Word says if you break one commandment you have broken them all. Again, the Word says Jesus is the way, the truth and the life, no one will see God without going through Him and that all those who accepted Him, He gave them power to become children of God. It is said that God does not compromise on His Word. Prayer, Holy Spirit, help me to do everything what your word commands me to do without compromise. Amen. *9th February 2013*

CHAPTER THIRTEEN
THE DAY I WILL WALK TO HEAVEN

I IMAGINED the day I will walk to heaven to meet the Lord, forgetting all things on the earth. A word came to me that when the love of mankind is full for God, and when God's love is full for mankind it exceeds the love of a bride who is going to get married to a most handsome man, and bridegroom who is going to marry a most beautiful virgin bride. I worship you God. *26th February 2013*

CHAPTER FOURTEEN
PEOPLE LOSE THE JOY OF LIFE

PEOPLE OF GOD Are destroying themselves, I was deep asleep in meditation of the goodness of the Lord when this message came to me that "The People of God are destroying themselves." Before people destroy themselves, the enemy drives them into losing interest in living, they develop the attitude of I do not care what happens to me known as apathy. They become selfish not caring of even for their own children or anything happening around. They live in this I do not care attitude.

I had a relative whom I used to love very much, I shared with her until she came to know the Lord, but one time when got a disease of typhoid she started a fast of 7 days in the midst of heavy medication. Later the enemy brought her hallucinations that the Lord was coming for her. She had very little children and the youngest was two years.

She died in that state of selfishness not caring what would happen to her family. Her husband completely hated God and died a drunkard claiming that God was unfair. When the enemy wants to destroy people, he makes them lose the excitement of living. Life in the Lord is exciting because all the time you are expectant of what God is going to do next. In this state of losing excitement and eagerness, a person becomes dull, he does not have the drive of eagerness and enthusiasm for going into adventures of life.

People lose the joy of life. God created us to enjoy living on this earth and that is why he created every good thing to bring us joy. The sun, moon and stars, fish of all colours in the water, flowers, animals of all shapes, sizes, and prints. Whenever we see the things God created they bring us joy. In this case when a person has lost the joy of living, they no longer observe any beauty in anything. When the enemy wants to destroy people, he makes them lose hope. People live by hope, where there is no hope, people perish, when the sick person loses hope in himself he dies. Hope keep people focused ahead expecting something is going to happen soon even if it takes long to come, e.g. an HIV/AIDS patient may live because the scientists promised that they have discovered the drug which cures AIDS. So, people destroy themselves when they become less expectant, they say whatever comes, let it come.

We need to live expectantly, especially as Christians, we have heard now and then that our Lord is returning soon. Whenever you hear a big bang when it is threatening or about to rain, you look up thinking that the Lord might come and leave you.

People who are about to destroy themselves, they are so forgetful, even they start forgetting the day they are living in, they tell you even I no longer follow the dates of the month and days of the week. They are living in darkness. The enemy steals peace from his victims he wants to destroy. A person gets no peace about anything. Without peace you cannot get along with any one because you see everyone is against you.

A person without peace is full of fear and you are so scared to the extent of running from yourself. The enemy puts regrets in their lives and causes them not to be grateful to what God has done. In life God does a lot of good things for us to be thankful, even that life you are sitting in to regret is God given. They regret the day they were born, why they were born in that family, why they got married, why they had children, why they took that job, why?

Why? to everything, even: "why are they living?" At this stage that person starts talking, and looking at death instead of life, then the enemy approaches after putting you where he wanted you. He introduces you with a lump in your breast you run for a biopsy and they tell you, a development of cancer. After eating a hearty meal he feels a stomach ache to go to see a doctor and he tells him you are not going back you have an intestine abstraction, you have to be admitted for operation, and the next day he is gone.

Therefore, you find the enemy has prepared the victim for a long time for death. All along the enemy talked the victim into rejecting himself which brings in hatred for self. Denial and hatred block your hope to live. Once the victim has rejected himself and hates himself this brings self-judgment which results in self-condemnation "I am good for nothing even if I die, I do not regret."

When someone says it, the enemy has won. Children of God, if the worldly people who live in the kings or ruler's palace, they live under the subjection of our God. People who live around kings and rulers live in such excitement that you see them how they run and jump in excitement because they are with the king or president. All the time expecting something, whether good or bad, but they keep focused ahead. Then what about us, the children of the King of kings, why do we walk with our head down?

I worked in high offices, office of the Prime Minister, Office of the Vice President and Office of the President Idi Amin. Since 1973, soon when I left Uganda College of Commerce (UCC). Before he was ousted, I was working for his Chief Protocol officer; but what I observed was his body guards lived in 24hours of excitement, yet at times they faced death.

I remember one incident in 1976 when seated in the office with a young man who was his driver and mechanic and He was talking, laughing, putting on his khaki overalls looking good, ready to go to work, excited as usual then immediately the door opened and it was time to go. He jumped and off he went in about 10 minutes after living the office he was dead, we all heard a big bang.

As he was driving when they were about to reach the Police Barracks where Iddi Amin was going to pass out police officers, the asked Abbas to let him takeover and drive himself to the venue. After driving a few yards the jeep was blown off and the seat where Iddi Amin was supposed to be sitting, guess who was blown to pieces.

One of the smart army officers was trying to assassinate Amin, had hatched a plan on that day and planted a land mine; one smart police officer called Patrick Kimumwe was arrested for that incident. The children of God should have interest in all what we are doing and no spirit like "I do not care, selfish spirit." We have to care for our beloved ones, we have to have interest in life because we are not living for ourselves but for God and to fulfill His Will on earth.

How does one die a selfish death and leave a two-year-old child? Even king Hezekiah pleaded with God and He added him 15 years. Many times, people have gone to heaven by tricks of the enemy and the Lord asked them to come back, that it is not yet their time to go. *9th March 2013*

CHAPTER FIFTEEN
JUST ENOUGH TRUTH WITH FALSEHOOD

THE NEW AGE Plan to Defeat Christianity

Christianity is facing the greatest challenge in its history, a series of powerful and growing relaxation or calmness that are changing the quality of Bible interpretations and undermining the Faith of millions of people. Most Christians are scarcely aware of what is happening and much less do they understand the issue involved.

The relaxation or seduction is surprisingly easy. It does not take place as an obvious confrontational assault of rival religious beliefs that would be vigorously resisted Instead it comes to some Christians in the guise of faith producing techniques or tricks for gaining spiritual power and experiencing miracles (mbizayo - I return them) and for others as self-improvement psychology for fully realizing human potential.

Many have taken for granted the comfort zone of their churches and pastors. They are owned by the church and pastors even if there is proof that gay or homosexuality is in the church or done by their pastors who they will Fight nail and tooth. They do not realize that the Enemy is not outside the gate, he is within our midst. He has so infiltrated our churches that many people can no longer simply tell an enemy from a friend.

Pastors are preaching from heresy regarding receiving from God, e.g. plant a seed if you want to get married (kikwate, kitole). What's happening to our churches today? The New Age of disgrace. A time when many of our church leaders have embraced Positive Thinking and Faith Producing Techniques for gaining Spiritual Power.

In Uganda we have many Pastors who have become the biggest supporters of these heresies. They preach that Faith is a force that makes things happen if you believe they will, e.g. some youth have been claiming vehicles, houses, girls or boys they see and admire; so, in other words faith is not placed in God but power directed at Him.

For many evangelicals Faith no longer requires God as it is object, but is touted as positive power of the mind that creates whatever we want. Thus what we pray for my will to come to pass, not if God wills; because many time when we pray God says Ok Take, Wait or No. At times I have prayed for something and it happened there and then but when I prayed for Peter, Jesus said after 20 years he will return, and for Robert, Jesus said wait, and when I prayed for my relative who had AIDS to be cured Jesus said, "No" and she died.

One day listening to the radio I heard someone preaching that your unconscious mind ... has power. That when you pray even unconsciously things will happen. That you have power that turns a wish into reality when the wishes are strong enough. This reality is what sorcerers have been and are doing for ages. If you imagine certain thoughts or speak certain words and think that God must respond in a certain way you have slipped into sorcery; if not sorcery you are trying to play God or to manipulate God.

The Ascended Master theology which includes magical

powers like teleporting, levitating, and walking through walls now includes positive thinking and positive faith that has slipped into churches years ago. It is dominant among newer theologies teaching that you are able to create your own reality or change the development of one's soul to experience self-chosen things as they reach into higher levels and realms of so called "Christ Consciousness."

Some refer to it as positive thinking, others call it Angelology, and still others the New Age. Many innocent Christians have fallen into these teachings because they totally trust their pastors and they do not search for themselves. Pastors are not angels, also they can perceive things wrong, they copy teachings from each other, they have busy schedules and have no time to do research themselves, seek the Holy Spirit for guidance or scratch for themselves which has led many pastors to err.

There is no room for magic in a Christian's life where it is plainly a pseudonym for sorcery and worldly musicians who compete to be considered that they are greater than someone else. Also, pastors are competing to be considered great preachers, miracle workers or one who pulls a great crowd. In God there is no greater than ... When they do this, they are consistently promoting New Age propaganda preaching Man's own will above God's.

New Agers have been preaching that line for years. The underlying theme is that by creating your own reality and living in your own dream world there would be no thoughts of sin, accountability, and judgment. How one can make the world into anything he or she chooses through the power they already have within them with no thought of placing God's will above your own as you conjure up visions of materialistic possessions under the guise of faith.

Persuaded by such false teachings, Christians begin to see prayer as a religious way of getting their own ways, and they neglect it and set their own sights upon what they want, then try to short cut the way of faith to make it happen. They attend Seminars of Kikwate, Kitole known as blab and grab it, where they are taught "How to Write Your Own Ticket with God" by thinking certain thoughts, speaking certain words or visualizing goals.

These seminars are eagerly attended by thousands. This is New Age "faith." This faith is known as visualization, guided by imagery and witchcraft. Visualization and guided imagery have long been recognized by sorcerers as the most powerful and effective way to contact the spirit world and demons for supernatural powers and knowledge. New Agers have claimed for years that we can bring anything we want to into existence through visualization, e.g. good health and success, because we can create our own reality.

It is one of the fastest ways into the occultic imposing your own will upon God and other people. These mind manipulating techniques for creating health, wealth, or spiritual power are not new and they have always been a part of the occult. It is simply a devise by Satan to get a person to trust in their own imagination rather than God's word.

The Apostle Peter said, "Humble yourselves, therefore, under the mighty hand of God that He may exalt you at the proper time," 1 Peter 5:6. Positive thinking or positive Christianity has no room for sin, repentance, or guilt. In fact it is merely occultism dressed in Christian language virtually taking over America.

Those who promote positive thinking, possibility thinking, and positive confession is among the most influential church leaders and preachers in the country. New Agers know that the word "positive" is a catch-all word. If they said what they really meant, "damnable thinking" and "damnable confession" they would not have half the success they are enjoying amongst themselves today deceiving many Christians worldwide.

Robert Schuller's Cathedral was put on sale and purchased by the Catholic Church. Almost any positive belief supports the delusion or lies of infinite human potential while throwing in self-esteem, and self-worth which are concerned with social justice through humanistic efforts. The Kingdom Mandate beliefs of some denominations play into this facade as well including discernment for the kingdoms of darkness, self = DNA, or God.

THE LORD IS NOT WAITING FOR US TO BUILD HIS KINGDOM ON THIS EARTH.

However, Satan is. When the real Messiah returns, He is coming with a sword to judge and destroy, and not until the wickedness on earth is consumed will He build His own reign here on earth. Today we are also seeing an increase in the preoccupation with "self" where humility is out and self-esteem is in contrary to I Peter 5:6. When Scripture speaks of self it usually commands self-denial and self-control and condemns self-worship.

It does not teach self-love, self-assertion, self-esteem, or self-forgiveness, instead it teaches us to turn ourselves to Christ Jesus who said we are to deny ourselves and take up His cross, Matt. 16:24-25, and not to be self-seeking. The message of success and self-esteem has become so important in the church today it has taken the place of sound doctrine, which for many seems too radical and old fashioned to be taken seriously in this day and age.

Christ said that He came to call "sinners to repentance" yet the churches are not preaching repent and stop sinning. It has been replaced with feel good theologies and things that are positive, e.g. marriage, visas to travel, buildings, purchasing land, building big churches, etc. Sin is so negative it keeps people away and doesn't fill the coffers. The self-help teaching theologies in the churches today are deceiving millions who are perhaps, unknowingly placing themselves above God. The only correct self-image comes from viewing God, not ourselves, and it isn't flattering, but it changes lives and turns us from ourselves to Him. So, God created man in his own image, in the image of God created he him; male and female created he them, Genesis 1:27.

Today such Biblical truths are considered psychologically damaging to one's self-esteem. No, it's not an outward assault on Christianity that the New Agers are seeking, for now they are succeeding quite well with their inward subversion of New Age doctrine and philosophy into Christian theology. Invading our churches at an alarming rate also are Positive Mental Attitudes and Human Potential techniques. These leaders teach that we can become masters of our own fate, that we should have self-confidence and faith in ourselves.

Who needs God? Their underlying message is that man can obtain his own godhood without indicating that this is sorcery and that God cannot be manipulated through mental thought processes. There is no room for sin or repentance in these methods either. Today's Christianity resembles more of humanism which wants us to believe in human potential and self-deification rather than God. It is no surprise then to learn that the Human Potential Movement and the New Age Movement are both indeed the same movement.

They are both the same just carrying separate titles. It has become the fastest growing movement in the world underlying many theologies and denominations today. Other New Age doctrines which have been accepted into our churches include Positive Confession in which we are all gods and that man is the god of this earth.

A televangelist has also become established all over the country, they instruct wealthy and independent Christians that they can take over the world for Christ.

There are many religious leaders falling prey to the New Age and many more occult themes being reworded as Christian theology and then indoctrinated into our churches despite the fact that these New Age beliefs are contrary to scripture, demeaning to God's attributes, and defamatory.

Many of our most celebrated churches today characterize the Laodicean Church of Revelations 3:14-22 who are wealthy and in need of nothing. These religious leaders influence millions around the world everyday leading them into doctrines of devils. They collectively preach that it is unnecessarily negative and to worry and preach about sin and repentance and that one can use faith to get what he or she wants by manipulating God.

They say that the world is on the road to international revival towards Christ and this is contrary to what the Bible teaches that the latter days will be as the days of Noah and the church completely apostate and falling away. This revival in Christ is not our Jesus but the Antichrist. Many are being attracted into Christianity today because of the false teachings and new Christ who has the attributes of Antichrist. They are being fooled into thinking they are following the true Gospel when in fact, wolves are leading them astray.

Many of our church leaders are not teaching Jesus Christ but the Christ portrayed in New Age propaganda that no longer calls sinners to repentance and excuses ungodly behavior as a psychological problem resulting from traumas suffered in childhood. Instead of requiring his disciples to "deny self and take up the cross," he teaches them to love and accept themselves and to recognize their inherent self-worth. Nor does this "Christ" promise the meek that they will inherit the earth, but offers self-assertion training.

Instead of blessing those that mourn he warns against low self-esteem and promotes a new positive self-image. And rather than promising heaven to the poor in spirit, this false Christ offers to the financially poor the enticing gospel of a hundredfold return for gifts to certain ministries. This Christ who is being presented and redefined is not our Jesus Christ but a blasphemous counterfeit and deceiver ready and waiting to take over the world. He is the antichrist who is blinding the eyes of men and women from seeing the counterfeit, he is and turning them away from Jesus the Most Highest.

Prophetic scholars know that the world must be primed both religiously and politically to embrace the Antichrist when he suddenly rises to power. If Christianity is to be the official world religion, which must be the case if the antichrist claims to be Christ, then it must be blasphemous enough to accommodate all of the world's faiths.

DO NOT BE DECEIVED, THIS IS NOT TRUE CHRISTIANITY

Do not be deceived, this is not true Christianity preaching a message of salvation but a perverted form that is already invading our churches today with little resistance from its members. In fact, the message of the cross is being rejected!

And that was the biggest sign of apostasy and the end of the age as given to us by prophetic Yahushua and His apostles. And, there is no stopping the exploding and relentless Ecumenical Movement led by mostly liberal, unbelieving leaders who have secretly taken masonic and Jesuit oaths, and who serve as pastors today.

Many of our church leaders are spearheading the antichrist's arrival by accomplishing exactly what he needs. That is a unification of all religions and they are succeeding through rallying cries of "peace and unity." Even a prophetic self-acclaimed guru has Catholic and world unity agenda for the Ecumenical. Though their cry for unity is tempting, it denies the true Christ and is a unification that will ultimately lead to destruction.

Many of our evangelical leaders are promoting ecumenicism alongside the rest of the world, people who neither accept the literal interpretation of the Bible nor take heed to God's warnings of compromising our faith for doctrines of devils and rejecting God's Truths.

UNITY IS CERTAINLY SOMETHING WE SHOULD STRIVE FOR AMONG MANKIND, BUT NEVER AT THE EXPENSE OF BIBLICAL TRUTHS AND DOCTRINES.

The death, burial, and resurrection of our Jesus would make any kind of union with the world's religions both impossible and abominable, this would lower our Lord's status to the same level as Buddha, Muhammad, and Confucius among others recognizing them all as great leaders. It is what they do not tell their church congregations that make these ecumenical leaders among our churches all the more dangerous. Perhaps, these leaders are unknowingly being deceived themselves, but a union of all the world's religions will be a crushing, stumbling block to the true Christian church who will no longer be able to preach the Word of God as openly as we can now. In a tolerant world all is one and one is all.

To criticize the deception of a religion would be intolerable. To preach your views against someone else's views would be considered a crime against the establishment therefore in a tolerant ecumenical world Jesus Christ would just be another great leader. His ministry would be no greater than a guru. The Bible would be the same as an encyclopedia of historic events. Is this really what our churches want?

Yet it is prophesied that this will come to pass and every Christian must decide what stand he will take. The Bible teaches that if Jesus isn't Lord of all, He isn't Lord at all. Yet those who oppose this ecumenicism are labeled as "narrow minded bigots" for uncompromising the Truth that Scripture warns we are not to sell at any price, Prov. 23:23, or barter for a delusional peace and unification. Many Christians are being deceived by the New Agers commitment to love and peace. They can't believe that anyone who is committed to love and peace could actually be an instrument of Satan.

Precisely, why Jesus warned us that Satan can pose as an angel of light and transform his demons into ministers of perceived righteousness. Do not be deceived, Satan, an angel of light, is shining his light through many of our churches today. For religious leaders who claim to know the Bible, one would think they would be the first ones to know when they are being deceived, that they would be the first to recognize religious deception.

However, satan knows in order to destroy the Christian Church he has to start from the top down and kill it with subversion and bribes, which is an amount of money given to a person by government or organization. Satan is quietly succeeding. The appeal of New Age doctrines is that they offer a new way of perceiving reality and religion.

THIS POSES A TREMENDOUS CHALLENGE TO TRUE BELIEVERS.

The New Age is more than a passing fad, it offers spiritual reality, fulfillment, and world harmony. Yet it has promises that spring from what turns out to be spiritually counterfeit. New Agers know that Christians will not accept a frontal assault of occultic doctrines and themes, so they changed occultic words into Christian terms such as Faith, God, Christ, and Born Again with many churches buying it hooks, line, and sinking.

Satan knows how to mix just enough truth with falsehood to make the falsehood seem true and intensely appealing. He already has millions falling into his traps of destruction. Do not be deceived and if you have been deceived get out of the deception. Return to and stay focused on the Most High.

These new formed groups may be more than passing fads offering spiritual reality, fulfillment, and world harmony yet the promises spring from what turns out to be a spiritual counterfeit. Scripture repeatedly warns us of spiritual counterfeits, warnings of counterfeit Christians (Matt. 24:5; Acts 5:36-37), counterfeit prophets (Deut. 13:1-4; Matt. 7:15; 24:11), counterfeit miracles (Ex. 7:8-13), counterfeit angels, counterfeit gods , counterfeit good works (Matt. 7:15-23), counterfeit godliness (2 Tim. 3:5), counterfeit converts (1 John 2:19; 2), counterfeit spirits (1 John 4:1-3), counterfeit doctrine (1 Tim. 4:1-3) and counterfeit gospels.

New emerging group leaders know that Christians will not accept a frontal assault of occultic doctrines and themes, so they changed occultic words into Christian terms such as "faith, God, Christ, and born-again" with many churches buying it hooks, lines and sinking. Satan knows how to mix just enough truth with falsehood to make the falsehood seem true and intensely appealing. He already has millions falling into his traps of destruction. Do not be deceived and if you have been getting out of the deception.

Return to and stay focused on the Highest. *23rd March 2013*

The farm

Maize from the farm

CHAPTER SIXTEEN
JESUS IS THE REASON WHY I LIVE

CLARE'S DREAM. I was standing at the podium wearing the most beautiful and powerful medal. An anthem was played and the medal was in built with the anthem which would be translated into beautiful music which would circulate the music into the spirit. When I looked for her to stand for the anthem she was still wearing the old pearls behind the medal which annoyed me and I grabbed it off her neck and rebuked her. *28th March 2013*

MORNING PRAYER FROM 3.36-5.42AM. THREE VOICES, FIRST voice, my prayers for Man's obedience doing the Will of God the creator. Second voice. the cock was crowing, so the creature was doing what God created it to do. Third voice, the Moslem man's disobedience of refusing to honour God and worshiping the devil. They were all at the same time raising voices. *28th March 2013*

Message, I arrived home in the village and in vision heard that: When she was in the kitchen washing dishes the Lord said

"I have changed your destiny." I asked "Who is this, Lord?" 4th April 2013

In prayer the Holy Spirit put it on my heart that I was scattered, I was a worn out rug, it is the Lord who collected me and put me together. Before I met the Lord, I was scattered all over the place or places my thoughts were everywhere, not knowing what to do next, or all what I was doing was wrong in the sight of God.

This is because I was doing my own desires and wishes. I was flesh, self-driven in evil, where ever I wanted to go, I went. Whatever I wanted to say I would say without self-checking and editing my words spoken in a day, or what I said or spoke to someone. I did not mind whether I had hurt him or her or if I said it I would be gratified that yes she or he deserved it.

I was scattered and all the good seeds the Lord had created to plant for goodness were all scattered in different directions, some were rotting at the backyard, others had germinated in the garbage pit, others the birds had carried them far and dropped them in the forest. Others were taken (by omugezi) and they grew in the backyard heap without nutrients, these seeds grew so tall and transparent with long vines, they do not bring flowers and no fruits or seeds. These type of seeds you find planted in people even though they have known the Lord but because there were some issues from family background, ancestors, grandparents and parents, broken curses, contracts, agreements and or covenants and these issues which were not repented.

These will continue tiptoeing, following you, even if you pray, fast, and have hands laid on you still need to be disentangled from these bondages. All my seeds were scattered in wrong areas Before the Lord found me, I was a worn out rug, there was nowhere to patch me together, and where ever you passed a needle thread it would separate and make a gaping hole.

My life was so worn out, even if you tried to hold me

together, only pieces would remain in your hands. I could not be held together, but when the Lord came to me all things were put together. The seeds which were scattered we all collected together and put in a beautiful tin and given my name. My rugged life was put together, now it can be sown together. *9th April 2013*

Message, I received this message when I was traveling from the village to Kampala.

When I read a message that one of our government ministers Dr Malinga had dropped dead without being sick then in my heart I asked myself how have I survived all this time, I found out that because Jesus is the reason why I live.

I am like drop of water on smooth leaf shaken by every situation and condition. Jesus Christ the Son of God is the reason why I live. Without Him at the blink of an eye I would be gone, but it is By His Grace I am living. There had been many chances the enemy had to take my life but the Lord stood in and gave him no opportunity. It's not easy to hold water on smooth surface of a leaf.

So in this world we are living in it is like we are drop of water hanging on a smooth leaf and there many chances for this bead of water to roll over the leaf and drop down. On this leaf where we are hanging there many situations which can make us roll over: the wind, a passerby, a bird lighting on the leaf or a bee coming to collect pollen from another plant can shake the leaf and that water on the leaf drops off to the ground. There are diseases like AIDS, heart attacks, cancers of every kind, high and low blood pressures, and diabetes to name but a few.

There are accidents. I live in Uganda, the land where I survived many wars, there were many senseless wars and AIDS and all these killed multitudes and multitudes of people, but I was spared on that leaf. When we come to know the Lord He steadies the situations which shake the leaf. We need to have more of Him in us.

We need to live only for Him daily, forget completely ourselves, surrender our lives, even when time comes and one wants your head you will surrender it, saying like Shadrach, Meshach and Abednego who said: if He saves us it's ok but even if He does not save us, we will not worship your idols king!!! And they entered the fire. We need to reach such level as we are still on the leaf. Total surrender, and that is when He is going to entrust us with His treasures.

Our Lord is looking for whom He can send. The days are evil and tense with every calamity aiming to destroy man. Winds, storms, tornadoes, hurricane, and a tsunami I saw on live broadcasts 2011.

When I was in Virginia the river Potomac in Washington, DC over flowed its banks and people in kayaks were swept by the rapids of water but one woman by luck got to hold on to a tree branch and froze there until when the rescuers came and picked her.

We were in a living room praying for her not to let go or fall off. Jesus is the reason why live. She had dropped from a leaf but the Lord could not let the drop touch the ground. Many of us have reached a desperate situation where the water on the leaf had started rolling and was caught at the edge of the leaf and the hand of the Lord held it there. *13th April 2013*

CHAPTER SEVENTEEN
OPPORTUNITY TO GIVE... SO THAT HE CAN BLESS THEM

MESSAGE, The word of the Lord came to Jeremiah, Behold, I am the Lord, the God of all flesh. Is anything too hard for me? Jeremiah 32:26, 27 (ESV).

I woke up to pray. Since I visited Bufunjo land at Kataraka with Sam Biryegira and Nathan Karwani on 11th April 2013 twice I had been dreaming about the land, soon when we returned I slept and dreamt about demons and strong holds at Kataka. When I woke, I prayed and bound them. This 14th day the Lord showed me the land across and the forest. I am seeing how the Lord has given me that land for His glory. So, when I opened the Bible already to Jeremiah 32 and how he is purchasing the land. *14th April 2013*

I LEFT UGANDA FOR USA, ARRIVED IN MARYLAND AT A sister's on 17th when she met me at Dulles Airport. *16th April 2013*

AT A FRIEND'S HOME, AFTER SHARING COLOSSIANS, THEY asked me why I was asking people for money to put up the teacher's quarters, scholarships for the children and a milling machine, yet the Lord has been financing most of the needs I have. I answered that the Lord was not looking at somebody only in this room, but He can use somebody anywhere who is willing to plant a seed in His work.

In the morning the Lord spoke to me that "the Lord was giving people opportunities to give in His Work so that He can bless them." A few days after He said that people think that blessings are only financial, but blessings come in spiritual blessings, physical blessings and or material blessings. He said people here are financially and materially blessed, He is giving them opportunity to give in His work so that He can bless them. *22nd April* 2012

I ARRIVED AT DALLAS AND LORENA MET ME AT FORT WORTH Airport. When we met for dinner with Pastor Dennis and Sis Loraine, we were sharing about lost souls and the Lord's coming.

MY PEOPLE ARE NOT SERIOUS, THEY ARE PLAYING GAMES, GO TELL THEM I AM COMING SOON

I told them that the Lord, one time with urgency in His voice said: "My people are not serious, they are playing games, go tell them I am coming soon." Then Loraine said that she also got the same message. Then the Lord told pastor Dennis that He is and has been coming every day for million's souls, and most of the souls are not going to Him but getting lost.

This has changed the course of my prayer life and since 2007 I started to pray for souls in every continent, now I am praying for one million souls living every day to meet the Lord from every continent. I asked the Lord to lay more burdens on my prayer life to intercede for these souls to be redirected to the Lord. *28th April 2013*

I WENT TO SEE THE DENTIST AND SHE FOUND MY BLOOD pressure was 220 and 230/110. They were alarmed because I could be in a sorry state, but I was as normal as any person could be. She refused to work on me because she said she wanted to pluck two teeth which was going to leave me with a terrible devastating state. Inside of me I said, No, this cannot happen. She sent me to go to see a medical doctor.

When we went to Family Care Clinic nearly everybody fell in love with me because they were born-again believers. When they took my pressure again but there was no change and they wanted to admit me but they could not as I was having no sign of being in danger. When they came to take my blood, we found out that she was going to the church of Pastor David Platt, Sis Judy earlier shared with me that she wanted to know who goes to his church. Immediately she called her husband and he brought me two of the books by pastor David Platt. God is amazing!!! *15th May 2013*

WITH SICKNESSES AND DISEASES, THROUGHOUT MY SPIRIT I was in battle of how God created man to be in good health, but the enemy introduced sicknesses and diseases in our bodies. The Lord said Be Holy as I am Holy, how can He allow this in our bodies where He resides. We need to know who we belong and claim His healing power. We need to be wholly body and spirit. I was laughing all the time in the doctor's office when they said my blood pressure was 230/110 and I was feeling nothing in my body.

The dentist said that my host should rush me to the doctor before I collapse or get a stroke, but I was still at peace and smiling. The enemy can run to the doctor's office and disorganize the machines to make you panic so that you can change your confession. The Lord paid it all, in sleep I was cleansing myself of all the diseases the enemy had introduced in my body. *17th May 2013*

I AM STILL GOING THROUGH THE SAME EPISODES OF HIGH blood pressure and pains of all kinds in my body and telling no one, but I know this is the greatest battle which started in January and up to now but I am bound to win. *19th May 2013*

I WOKE UP AT 3.00AM AT IN CALIFORNIA AND THE WORD IN my heart was the Medal. Many people leave this world after winning a World Cup at the Olympic games with different Medals after running, jumping, swimming, dancing, etc. We Christians know our medal is going to be earned based on how many souls we are going to bring to our Lord before we leave this world. What medal are you working out to receive when we get to His presence? *22nd May 2013*

CHAPTER EIGHTEEN
TRIALS ARE COMING TO PEOPLE OF GOD IN A WHIRLWIND

TRIALS WHICH COME in like a whirl wind, Coming from Deborah Sharp, Jennifer showed me the former Ranch property in Palmdale, California. After walking a few yards, I remembered that Sis Agnes was removed from there in a whirl wind style. LAX owned the property and wanted to expand the airport facility; but up to now it has never come to pass.

I turned to Jennifer and told her that there were no planes except the Lord wanted to remove Sis Agnes and bless her with a newer bigger facility like no one could dream. As a result of all that Sis Agnes got a massive stroke and was hospitalized as she could not handle the situation. Sis Teresa was used in such a mighty way to secure a house beyond anybody's imagination.

There will be trials which are coming to people of God in a whirl wind style and they call them misfortunes, yet they have come to lift us from a miserable situation into a glorious situation. At times it can even be death. In my testimony I always share that young as I was at 32 years old all the three fathers of my kids were dead. The father of Robert was murdered by Idi Amin in 1973, the father of Clare was murdered by Obote's regime in 1980, the father of Peter and Emma died of brain tumor in 1982, and then Peter was kidnapped when he was two years only to return after 22 years,.

In 1982 after walking with the Lord two years I was still a baby Christian when I asked the Lord what had I done to deserve these 1985 terrible, terrible things that started happening again and over again. The small special hire car which we used to bring us milk and food was taken at gunpoint on 16th February 1986 as soon the forces from the Bush War of Yoweri Museveni entered the city.

This trial was so bad as it brought in a lot of suffering physically, spiritually and materially. I was tried along with my children, many times we counted how many meals we had eaten in a month as we used to go without food for so many days and even water was bitter to drink. Robert was young and Emma who was in kindergarten as their strength failed them many times so they never went to school.

Emma became so malnourished his legs bowed. I was suffering in the midst of plenty. No one can understand how one working in the office of the president could go for days without food, this was unheard of. The Lord brought me this whirl wind in the midst of plenty. Every Tuesday was a Cabinet day so in the office they used to bring a banquet table where all the Secretaries on the third floor were asked by Cabinet Secretary George Sabiiti to go and eat as much as we could take in. Really, how could I eat on a king's table while my kids were having no food or had gone three to four days without food. Clare would hock her clothes so that she could bring something to eat at home.

In 1986 I was working with the Minister of State for Security Hon Balaki Kirya. Due to the torturers he went through when he was dragged all the way from Nairobi to Luzira Prison, he was brought in the boot of a car and he had lost part of his memory. Many times he would open a safe full of foreign currency still in bundles from the bank, and there I would enter and stare at all the money and the enemy would tell me "nobody is here to see you just pick a few £s and go and feed your children." I would run and lock the safe and walk away home empty handed and at home found the children still sleeping on the floor as I left them. The Lord used to give me strength to walk to the office and back without fainting on the way.

Whirlwinds of other people I know, Loy Bangirana, Josephine Katuramu, and Gertrude Kabatalemwa. 27th May 2013

CONFIRMATION, WE WENT TO VISIT KIM ETTER'S SCHOOL with Sis Teresa. After talking to children in Sis Gerry Grades 4 and 5, one young boy came out and asked me "How old are you?" and I told him "I am 66 years old." He said "Wow! you are not even walking in a wheel chair. You look 51 years old!" This is what some time back I asked to reverse me of 15 years old; however I was thinking 66 - 51 = 15 years old and not 51 years. 28th May 2013

CHAPTER NINETEEN
HOLY SPIRIT PREPARE US FOR THE MARRIAGE SUPPER

AFTER LUNCH with the Pastor we went to pray with with some people, one who looked like a bum, but he could sing his heart out with tears in his eyes as he touched everybody's heart. He stays by himself in a house without power or water and lives on very little supplies. Sis wanted to start giving him food but he refused and said he was well supplied and that at times he comes home and find supplies at his door.

We went in to pray for a brother who was suffering from cancer with his stomach so swollen and in great pain. I led him to repentance and he accepted the Lord. Then, I prayed for him and Sis Nannette gave him a word of wisdom and then he prayed with his wife.

Next, we went in to pray for a woman, the enemy made her mute so she could not talk because her neck muscle collapsed. The Lord gave a word and also many prayers were said over her, but I prayed for her for only this time. I prayed for her according to what the Lord led me. Back at the cabin I asked the Lord for a word the man. The Lord said "what you have decided to give him is the Word for him." I called him and gave him my $100 and we left.

Message of the preparation of a bride came to me while I was in the house of Sis Nannette and Bro Lenny in Rusburg.

So, the Lord spoke to me about the bridal preparation, both families would be involved in the talks. The bridegroom and the bride did not know each other until the day of the wedding. The both sides would try to spy each side to know what idol they were ascribing to, e.g. embandwa eyera or embandwa iragura; and what disease they suffered, e.g. epilepsy, cancer, TB, leukemia, etc.

When they found out that the other family was having bad idolatry spirits the marriage was cancelled. When they found out that there was nothing serious the girl's parents accepted the dowry and went ahead to prepare for the wedding. The girl's side would start preparing the girl for marriage.

A principle aunt would be summoned to come start the rituals of preparing the girl for her new home. Other aunts or friends of her mom would also come to prepare her in Skin care, includes the processing of her special cream that commences when cow's gee which was hanged very high over the fire place and it would leak drop by drop into a container.

After they would start putting scents from sandalwood powder from a particular forest (eseeta), seeds (eraza) the county where cows graze, and or from selected swamp's prat of dried papyrus plant (emyamirro). This cream was so fine and smelled so good and once used the whole house would smell good. The bride's skin was taken care of by scrubbing and washing with herbs and using the soil and clay from a red ant hill (orusasa from Omubarama) and that makes skin smoother until her whole body is like a baby's skin.

Inside cleansing where the aunt would every now and then cleanse her inside by giving her enema with herbs to completely clean her inside so that no bad air would come out of her bowels. Burners of incense so the women would collect scents to burn in the incense burners. This was used to expel bugs from the house, once burnt in the room all cockroaches, fleas and other insects could not stand the smell of sandalwood and other collected incenses.

The aunt would coach her in the language of the family she is going to marry. How they call different things, they would coach her not to mention certain animals, places, and intecils in the house if they portrayed the names of the house. The bride should hold names of her in-laws in respect, e.g. if one was named after the cow she would not mention a cow, if one was named after the mosquito she should not say that he was as small as a mosquito, or if one was named where he was born on the way (Bagenda, Kageda) she would not mention that place.

The aunt would coach her how to behave in her new home, e.g. not to answer back her husband, what to do when he became tired from a day's chore, etc. The bride learned that after when she got married in that home they would give her another name to cherish her, e.g. Kaboga meaning that she was so beautiful, Kagaga meaning she was slender as beautiful as a reed that grows in the middle of a sea, or maybe Kanyange meaning as beautiful as white ibis.

THE HOLY SPIRIT IS LIKE OUR AUNT TO HELP US TO PREPARE FOR THE MARRIAGE SUPPER.

So, if tribal people prepare a bride to that extent for her earthly marriage, what about our eternity home. The bride was cared for inside and outside. Jesus said that He is coming for a spotless church without a wrinkle or spot. His word does not change, He said it. It has to remain. We need to prepare ourselves inside out, so when Jesus comes again, He will find us spotless. The Holy Spirit is like our aunt to help us to prepare for the Marriage Supper.

He is teaching us the language we have to speak. In the kingdom of God our language is different. We do not swear in vain, we do not curse, we do not use profane language. The Holy Spirit is teaching us how to cleanse ourselves inside, our thoughts, wishes, expectations, anticipation and desires will be made clear.

We think evil, when a bad thought comes in we do not Fight it we savor it like the raven released from Noah's Ark found dead bodies and sat to eat and never returned; but the dove, because it is clean does not eat dead bodies, when it was released and did not find a place to rest returned to the Ark. Also, when our spirit wonders with bad thoughts and finds there is no place to rest we better not savor on dead bodies but return and the Holy Spirit will put out His hand and receive us back in God's peaceful place. The cleaning of the outside, the holy Spirit after cleaning the inside will illuminate the outside.

When the Lord in 1998 asked me why I was painting myself He said "Do you think that pencil adds to you any beauty? Why do not you seek the inside beauty?" The Lord wants our inside beauty first which is not seen by outside standards but only He Himself who sees the inside. He has a secret name for us. The one who conquers, I will make him a pillar in the temple of my God. Never shall he go out of it, and I will write on him the name of my God, and the name of the city of my God, the new Jerusalem, which comes down from my God out of heaven, and my own new name. *2nd June 2013*

CHAPTER TWENTY
"KOMUKITUURUKYE"

AT BRO and Sis Roland Beards, This came to me when I was on my morning prayer walk. There is no formal high education degree, no PhD, no Doctorate, no level of riches, no bodily size, no height or nor depth, and no black or white skin can put our souls to rest. Always there will be a vacuum, a hollow which will be unfulfilled. That is why presidents of this world stick to power, they think they want to get more and more, they have all the money they want and all the fame but they want to get more and more. The Lord requires us to prepare ourselves for His Return. He said He is coming for a church without a wrinkle or spot. Let us clean up inside and outside. *8th June 2013*

I LEFT AT 12.00PM NOON FOR DULLES AIRPORT IN Washington DC. Due to heavy rain we left Dulles at 8.00pm and arrived in Amsterdam at 8.30am and then left for Entebbe Airport at 10.45am.

On my flight to Amsterdam while praying for different families and individuals the Lord brought in the man we met in Rusburg with Sis Nannette. The man had searching, penetrating eyes and looked like a bum. His shoes were of a gentleman. He lived in an old truck so he told us. He said he fills a bathtub with water then puts down a glass door for the sun to warm it. He had no power and no water in his shelter and did not want them. He refused Sis Nannette offer to take food for him and he said he was well supplied. He sang a song for us "You Do not Know." The Lord impressed on me to give him an offering and the Lord asked Sis Nannette to hug him. *10th June 2013*

I RESTED.

Dream, I was sleeping on a big python as my pillow and my head was close to the mouth of a lion. All these dangerous and ugly creatures were surrounding me. The Holy Spirit told me not to be scared but pray and those creatures were silenced and made inactive. When I woke up a question was asked to me "what would you prefer, to sleep on a bed of roses or to sleep on the terrible ugly creatures? I answered on top of terrible creatures!!! This is because a power of being in prayer can silence such creatures and because many people would like to sleep on a bed of roses. This world is full roaring lions and seething pythons but we are overcomers. *13th June 2013*

DREAM, I SAW BIG PYTHONS, LIONS AND OTHER TERRIBLE creatures, animals just moving around, as sleeping on a big python as my pillow and my head was close to the mouth of a lion. All these dangerous and ugly creatures were surrounding me. I got scared but the Holy Spirit told me not to be scared but pray and those creatures were silenced and made inactive. The following day the witness inside me asked "Do you know that the world you are living in is full of dangerous animals and those are the powers of darkness? You are walking on mouths of lions, sleeping on pythons, etc." *14th June 2013*

NEW NAMES INCLUDE ETERNITY FACE AWARD AND THIS award is beheld by our Lord, Komukituurukye, Hakiire, and Tigalyoma. Since 15th in my prayers I kept crying and looking at the face of the Lord from the Passion of Christ. Whenever I see His face I wince avoiding and trying to keep my eyes on it. It hurts me to see what the Lord went through. This time as I was praying, I found myself in a vision rubbing my face on the bloody beaten face of Jesus no longer avoiding to look at it.

This continued all day as I was kissing the face of our Lord and I said there is no face which is so beautiful, this is the fairest face in heaven and on the earth. I called it the face which won the "Eternity Face Award." In my prayers I asked the for Lord's hand to overshadow me when I pray, meditate, and seek Him; and as I walk, talk, sleep or sit. Whenever arguments or differences arise, may the Lord's hand keep following and covering me wherever I move. Whenever I am under the shadow of His hand may the Lord correct errors and mistakes I make. Another name for me is "Komukituurukye" meaning "Who dwells in the Shadow of The Almighty." *17th June 2013*

MY MONEY IN THE HANDBAG WAS STOLEN, 780,000, FOR

which I released missiles, bombs and nuclear weapons of prayer. For three hours Nathan, Stella and I, we confronted the enemy. I could not sleep at all and my spirit was in His presence the whole time I was interceding asking the Lord to take over and use me.
22nd June 2013

CHAPTER TWENTY-ONE
ALL I WANT IS YOU JESUS

EARLY IN THE morning my Lord appeared in my spirit and started to talk through the song All I Want Is You.

He said He has come to stay. Wherever, whenever that I call on Him, He will be there. He will take me to king's and rulers of the world or bring them to me for counseling and answering their queries; then I saw my sandals running on the steps in 1980s. That the Lord will stand and give me pain, I will see Him as He is raised to Glory, I will see Him sitting in glory. That more people are going to hate me even to the point of killing me and those who call themselves His; but the sword of His mouth will come out and consume them. He said "I will no longer keep quiet." He said from now on He will not keep quiet. *23rd June 2013*

I READ THE QUEEN OF SHEBA'S VISIT TO KING SOLOMON, 2 Chronicles 9 as was emailed by Pastor Chuck Swindoll about doctrinal danger of substituting temporary blessings for eternal blessings. People are looking for worldly riches, fame, and prestige in this world which are temporary instead of looking for an eternal blessing which is everlasting life. The Lord said store your riches where there is no rats, cockroaches and rust can get them, Matthew 6:19.

There is personal danger in trying to impress someone instead of imparting the Word to someone. The people of God are trying to impress others and they are in competition, rivaling each other as to who has the biggest congregation, cathedral, mass choir, or loudest PA system. Why, they should instead be imparting the Word of God which will deliver souls from eternal damnation! Gospel musicians are singing songs that draw people to make them popular worldly musicians. They copy dressing styles and flash satanic signs used by the secular musicians.

There is economical danger of spending more money than you have. Men of God are competing with the worldly tycoons. They go to buy vehicles worth 700,000,000 with personal number plates, and this is with the money from poor people who give all what they have and go walking back home with an empty stomach.

There is psychological danger in believing your purchase will make things all right. Men of God believe that when they display riches it puts them in a position that they are more spiritual, they believe that these worldly riches portray spiritual riches.

Make Jesus Christ your aim: Consider him who endured such opposition from sinners, so that you will not grow weary and lose heart, Hebrews 12:3. For it is: Do this, do that, a rule for this, a rule for that; a little here, a little there, Isaiah 28:10. It is the little here, little there about differences what makes a difference. 26th June 2013

I WOKE UP AT 4.00AM.

Prayer, Lord, let my tears flow as I cry cleanse my inner man. Let my tears wash my bridal attire, when you come you will find my bridal gown pure and clean. Lord you laid me on the floor to sleep on my side in order to speak to me. I sleep on the floor with you, I turn with you and I wake up with you. You are my God. Every time when I sit crying let it be like a woman in labour pains ready to give birth to something great in the spirit which will touch every one of every language, colour and nation causing them to turn to you Lord. Amen.

Yet another time I declared that I will no longer wince on looking at the bloodied face of our Lord on the Passion of Christ, but I will always embrace it, and smear myself in that blood in the spirit. Let us rejoice and exult and give him the glory, for the marriage of the Lamb has come, and his Bride has made herself ready; it was granted her to clothe herself with fine linen, bright and pure for the fine linen is the righteous deeds of the saints, Revelation 19:7-8 (ESV).

The rapture of the church will happen anytime soon. Only holy and righteous brides will get raptured. In order to get rapture we need robes, not only do we need the garments of salvation, we also need the robe of righteousness, Isaiah 61:10. It is time to sincerely repent on a daily basis and pray continuously. Love Jesus with all your heart. Keep in the fullness of the Holy Spirit. I am here like in birth pangs, as of a woman who is in labour about to give birth. *27th June 2013*

CHAPTER TWENTY-TWO
STORE YOUR RICHES WHERE NO RATS... CAN GET THEM

I RETURNED from the village with Emma to wait for Dr Chad who was arriving on 1st July 2013 and coming to work on the children. *27th June 2013*

DURING THE SIEGE OF JERUSALEM DO NOT GO DOWN TO Egypt because God will be merciful, Isaiah 29 and 30.

Prayer, Your Word says that because He has loved us that is why I will fill you with life, John 3:16. Abraham, Isaac, Jacob and Joseph loved you so much and you gave them life and blessings. I have loved you at a very difficult time, a time of all kinds of witchcraft and idolatry of every nature with paganism at the highest. Amen.

In the evening we went to have dinner with Pastors at Serena Hotel, it was our first time to go to that hotel. While we were there once again another big miracle happened. When we were eating Peter and Sammy came and sat opposite our table; Sammy is the boy who grew with Peter in Ghana in the home that adopted Peter. We would not have met Sammy if it was not for the Lord bringing him to our way. *29th June 2013*

THE LORD'S COMING SALVATION AND CRUCIFIXION, ho has believed what he has heard from us? Even some Rabbis think that the Bible was made up and written by Christians after the death of Christ. And to whom has the arm of the Lord been revealed? Who has got this revelation? Who this seeks wisdom to understand it? For he grew up before him like a young plant, Jesus was born in human flesh and grew before His Father. and like a root out of dry ground; He was a plant with a fresh root in a land which was dead, the world without God is a dry and dead ground. He had no form or majesty that we should look at Him, born in a humble manger and grew in a carpenter's home He did not show off, and had no beauty that we should desire Him.

He did not display His true heavenly beauty, He was seen as a commoner. He was despised and rejected by men; even though He did all those miracles, men did not take Him seriously. a man of sorrows and acquainted with grief; He always pleaded with the Pharisees "if you do not believe in me at least believe in the works I do, He pleaded. and as one from whom men hide their faces. The Pharisees, they booed Him and considered that they were holier than Him because they kept the 10 commandments of Moses. He was despised, and we esteemed Him not. They called Him the carpenter's son.

Surely, He has borne our griefs. Yes, He was born to carry our sins, and carried our sorrows; and He carried our heavy loads of transgressions. Yet we esteemed him stricken; we rejoice in His punishment, smitten by God, and afflicted. He was beaten by God and punished on our behalf. But he was pierced for our transgressions; He was wounded for our many sins.

He was crushed for our iniquities; He was mashed for our wrongs and upon him was the chastisement that brought us peace, He was judged that we may be at peace with God. and with His wounds we are healed; with His many beating stripes we are spiritually and physically healed. All we like sheep have gone astray; All of us have got lost in sin, we have turned - every one - to his own way; many have got lost in witchcraft, idolatry and paganism, and the Lord has laid Him the iniquity of us all.

God put all our sins on His head. He was oppressed, and he was afflicted, He felt low, and He was so much hurt, yet he opened not his mouth; But He did not plead for Himself. Like a lamb that is led to the slaughter, He was like a lamb that is led to be killed and like a sheep that before its shearers is silent, like a sheep, He was humiliated. So, he opened not his mouth. He did not say anything. By oppression and judgment, he was taken away. Because of people's pressure and wrong judgments exerted on Him He was led away. And as for his generation, who considered at that time no one gave a second thought, to say by the way that He was cut off out of the land of the living, He was killed. Stricken for the transgression of my people? Beaten for sins of His people which they committed.

And they made His grave with the wicked people who hanged Him among the sinners. And with a rich man in his death, in the tomb which was made for Joseph of Arimathea, a rich man. Although he had done no violence, He knew no sin and there was no deceit in his mouth. He had never ever told a lie. Yet it was the will of the Lord to crush him; our Father's intention to chastise Him for us all he has put him to grief; He suffered our humiliation when his soul makes an offering for guilt and when His soul stood in place of our guilt.

He shall see his offspring; he shall prolong their days. He sees whom He has redeemed and gives them long life because they know Him. The will of the Lord who shall prosper in his hand.

He will prosper whatever their hands do. Out of the anguish of His soul He shall see and be satisfied when people turn from their wicked ways and accept Him. His will be done. By his knowledge shall the righteous one, my servant, make many to be accounted righteous, and he shall bear their iniquities. By His forgiveness and Grace many will become children of God, because He has carried all our sins on Himself.

Therefore I will divide Him a portion with the many, and He shall divide the spoil with the strong, because He poured out his soul to death.

Life in Christ is real. It is not plastic, it is not stained-glass, it is not saccharine, and it is not fantasyland. In all my years of walking with the Lord, I have yet to meet one Christian who has lived happily ever after.

On the other hand, I have met a great many significant saints who have endured affliction, loss, disappointment, setbacks, failures, and incredible pain through the years. And I have seen many of those same men, women, and adolescents cling to their joy, radiate hope, and sustain a winsome spirit even through heartache, even through tears, and even at death's door. *2nd July 2013*

I travelled to the village with Dr Chad a chiropractor who was going to go treat and work on the kids, teachers, Management and the community. *4th July 2013*

CHAPTER TWENTY-THREE
SIX THINGS TO PRAY FOR

I WOKE up at 5.13am saying Lord:

How can I get sleep when I haven't talked to my God who gives sleep? How can I get a rest when I haven't spoken to my God who gives rest?How can I get healed when I haven't talked to my God who is the healer?How can I talk to anybody else when I haven't talked to my creator?How can I laugh before laughing with my maker?How can I walk without walking with His presence?How can I cry tears without the one who wipes them away?How can I walk pure without the one who purifies me?How can I walk holy without the one who said be holy as I am Holy?

I prayed for every craft which was touched by my hands or passed through my office to North America and beyond to stand in every home, office, or church and may those people are wearing my necklaces be used by the Holy Spirit this is a point of contact for my prayer of salvation for those souls. This prayer based on the scripture that the people who know their God, will take action and will do great exploitation, Daniel 11:32.

On this day I paid Kusemererwa 4m ugs part of 9m ugs for the purchase of land which he bought from Shaban. 5th July 2013

Message, Proverbs 8 is all about Wisdom which is talking about Jesus Christ from the beginning of the world that He was the one who was beside the Father when He was creating the earth.

SIX THINGS TO PRAY FOR:

1. To walk daily with His Presence.
2. To Ask God to flash or torch my life whenever I grieve the Holy Spirit; to show me where there are stains and wrinkles on my pure garment which would cause me to lose the marriage supper; and to show me where I lost my way so that I may retrace my foot steps and walk back in His righteous ways.
3. To intercede for lost souls daily, and
4. To intercede for the persecuted churches.
5. To intercede for my country Uganda.
6. To pray for Israel's Peace.

8th July 2013

Message, Whoever walks in integrity walks securely, but he who makes his ways crooked will be found out, Proverbs 10:9 (ESV).

What the wicked dreads will come upon him, but the desire of the righteous will be granted. Proverbs 10:24 (ESV). The fear of the Lord prolongs life, but the years of the wicked will be short, Proverbs 10:27 (ESV).

The righteous will never be removed, but the wicked will not dwell in the land, Proverbs 10:30 (ESV).

Whoever is steadfast in righteousness will live, but he who pursues evil will die, Proverbs 11:19 (ESV). Be assured, an evil person will not go unpunished, but the offspring of the righteous will be delivered, Proverbs 11:21 (ESV).

The desire of the righteous ends only in good; the expectation of the wicked in wrath. Proverbs 11:23 (ESV).

Whoever brings blessing will be enriched, and one who waters will himself be watered. Proverbs 11:25 (ESV).

Whoever trusts in his riches will fall, but the righteous will flourish like a green leaf. Proverbs 11:28 (ESV).

The fruit of the righteous is a tree of life, and whoever captures souls is wise. Proverbs 11:30 (ESV). *10, 11th July 2013*

In the fear of the Lord one has strong confidence, and his children will have a refuge. The fear of the Lord is a fountain of life, that one may turn away from the snares of death, Proverbs 14:26-27 (ESV). *14th July 2013*

WE LEFT FOR THE VILLAGE AT 6.00AM ON THE WAY AT Mityana.

I learnt about the death of Edith Kaboyo's mother.

When I was praying on the way to the village with Emma in my prayer on the way I was talking about the presence of the Lord and it came to me that: the Presence of the Lord is with every one, as the wired house with Power except it needs one to put on the Switch and then the light will be there. So, the presence of the Lord is always with you except you need to switch on by turning to God in prayer. The presence of the Lord is with you always, like the Water in the tap and like until you open that tap. So, the presence of the Lord is always there with you. You need to open the tap.

The presence of the Lord is with you always like the Radio Station you want to listen to but until you turn your knob to that Station you will not be able to hear the message you want. Just turn the knob to the station you want. Do not keep turning to every station, otherwise you will find on other stations what you do not want to hear, but turn it to the station where there is the right message which enriches your soul. Therefore, the presence of the Lord is there 24 hours from the day you are born till as long as you live on the earth, except it is the lies of the devil which have kept you in ignorance and which have kept you in darkness.
16th July 2013

CHAPTER TWENTY-FOUR
OUR LIVES ARE WORTHLESS WITHOUT GOD

DREAM, I had a beautiful swimming pool around my house and there was a fish pond. After some time in the pond I noticed there were all types of big fish of rare colours swimming around and hippos started chasing them across the swimming pool which scared me and they were chasing fish to eat them. The pool looked so beautiful with snow mixed in blue and white surrounding the house and I was wondering about that rear beauty. Alisa and her children stood at the big swimming pool and she said I love this place. Also, I started walking in the water so first fearing the hippos and crocs and I jumped quickly on the steps of the house to enter and I was safe.

Then Alena Kagina also was staying around the vicinity of my house, she started asking me names of her children if they have a meaning: the first one is called On, I answered her that yes, there are short names I know like O and others from China, then she said the next one is Two, and the third child is Miu. I woke up.

Interpretation, it is spiritual, it is the world I am living in which is infiltrated with all kinds of evil and good, dangerous animals are chasing to eat good ones. Over yonder my house there is extraordinary beauty of God. At times I am scared of these animals who are the evil people, but I have my beautiful house securely built on the rock and close to the world, representing the world with all kinds of wickedness. Foreigners with their families are also coming to my house to enjoy the goodness of the Lord and commenting how beautiful my place is, because of the presence of the Lord. From my house there is no distance with evil, it is overflowing at my door steps and I have to jump to escape from it.

But highly placed people came to ask for advise from me and I give them appropriate answers where they are even doubting their own children's identity. *18th July 2013*

ON 8TH JULY I ASKED GOD TO FLASH OR TORCH MY LIFE whenever I grieve the Holy Spirit, to show me where there are stains and wrinkles on my pure garment which would cause me to lose the marriage supper. I asked Him to show me where I lost my way so that I may retrace my foot steps and walk back in His righteous ways. I kept prodding Him to torch my life.

The answer from the Lord came through Gonzaga on this day in a dream, that there seemed to be a party somewhere and I was going to attend that party. I asked Gonzaga to wash my van, that on the van he saw four posters which he did not read or know their meaning. The van was having an imbedded band surrounding it, and when he saw the van, it was clean and he kept wondering why I wanted it to be cleaned again.

Interpretation, The party means the marriage supper of the Lord is ready that we are getting ready Rev. 19:7-8. The posters show He has given me a new name no one else knows, Rev. 3. The imbedded band around the van is His protection. The van was clean and needed not to be cleaned again, the Lord has cleaned me, I do not need to cleaned again.

Kangume and myself started a three day fast; 12 hours for wickedness in Nyamabuga area. We were faithful to this commitment. *19th July 2013*

Prayer, I give glory to my God. Amen.

But when you trust the Lord God to give you the next step, when you wait in humility upon Him, He will open the doors of blessings and close doors of the evil ones, and you will get to rest and relaxation ... until He says "Go." *20th July 2013*

We had a good time of prayer from 5.00 - to 7.00am with the children at home. *21st July 2013*

Message, I got this from Chuck Swindoll's Insight for Living when I was going through Alan experience. For my thoughts are not your thoughts, neither are your ways my ways, declares the Lord. For as the heavens are higher than the earth, so are my ways higher than your ways and my thoughts than your thoughts, Isaiah 55:8–9.

He is, nonetheless, for us. He's on our side. Therefore, we take a giant leap forward in dealing with difficult people when we say "Thank You Lord, for this painful experience of being maligned, misunderstood, and mistreated." When David finally reached this point he was able to give thanks to God, even in the midst of ongoing personal strife 2 4*th July* 2013

IN THE NEWSPAPER OF 25TH IT WAS REPORTED WHEN THE oil Company comes to full operation the salary of the Executive Director will be 51,000,000/- per month. That, that is the highest salary in the country. 2 5*th July* 2013

IN THE MORNING WHEN I WAS PRAYING AFTER READING OF the 51m/- salary per month, it came to my mind when I read the book of Rick Joyner that the Lord told him that if you put all together the riches Of this world they cannot purchase a man's soul for a fraction of a second. Therefore, when we are here on the earth, there is no figure of treasure or money put together one person is worth if he or she does not know the Lord. Our lives are worthless without God.

Even if you earn a trillion, a killion, a lillion, every second your soul will perish. But if you work towards winning souls for the Lord, you are worth eternity. The Lord has let us to live on this planet not to work for riches of this world to enrich ourselves but to share it with the less unfortunate, the poor so that they will give glory to God. The Lord said that we should store our riches where there are no cockroaches, rats and rust, Matthew 6:19. 26*th July* 2013

CHAPTER TWENTY-FIVE
REORGANIZING OUR INNER MAN

I SPENT the day in the container with Prillar, Imani and Stella cleaning, clearing and reorganizing, I got so tired. After a good meal which Kangume planned for me we decided to pray.

In prayer the Holy Spirit revealed to me that this is how life should be, that a time comes where we have to start:

Cleaning our Inner Man, this is to check out what is dirty and wash it out, put it out in the open, so that the sun can shine on it and all the insects which do not like the sun will crawl out. Put the Inner Man out in the open so that the clean air can blow through and the dust will be blown out.

Clearing Inner Man, this is to throw out what is not needed. Our souls are so congested with a lot of junk, we need to throw unwanted, unnecessary, and behaviors. We are walking with things that cling on us. It is time to start throwing out dirty things you have been hanging on to for a very long time thinking that they are important yet they are not. Some look good to you but they are snares and traps for you because they bring back old memories before you were saved and these will leave you stained. Throw Them Out, Burn Them so that you have no more unneeded, unwanted or unnecessary remembrance.

Reorganizing our Inner Man this is putting what is first in first place, Prioritizing your life. The time has come to clean, clear and reorganize our lives because the Bride's time is Zero Time, He is close to your door. *27th July 2013*

SATISFACTION IN PRAISE, O GOD, YOU ARE MY GOD; earnestly I seek you; my soul thirsts for you; my flesh faints for you, as in a dry and weary land where there is no water. So, I have looked upon you in the sanctuary, beholding your power and glory.

David's lonely wilderness sanctuary left him thirsty and hungry, not only for food, but for meaningful interaction with his God. Because your steadfast love is better than life, my lips will praise you. So, I will bless you as long as I live; in your name I will lift up my hands. My soul will be satisfied as with fat and rich food, and my mouth will praise you with joyful lips.

As his song continues, David describes a second decision he made to cultivate a relationship with the Lord: he decided to express praise to the Lord. There's nothing mystical or mysterious about praising God. David tells us that praise is something we do with our lips, not merely our minds. We speak something out loud so that others, can hear our words of affirmation concerning the Lord, and just as important, so that we can hear these words. He says it is to be done "as long as I live," so it isn't a once-a-week matter. Moreover, where God's "lovingkindness" prompts David to praise his Lord, praise "satisfies his soul."

Yes, praise is a deeply significant aspect of our personal worship. Unfortunately, many are afraid of praise because they associate it with some sort of wild, uncontrolled, highly emotional "praise service" in which individuals faint, scream, jump around, and dance uncontrollably in the aisle. Listen, praise is important!

It is not limited to organized services. Praise is a consistent flow of appreciation for God in every circumstance throughout the day. Then, when we're alone, praise is an aspect of prayer.

Confession, dealing completely with sins in our lives, agreeing with God that such-and-such was wrong, then claiming forgiveness. Proverbs 28:13 and 1 John 1:9.

Intercession, and remembering others and their needs in prayer. 1 Timothy 2:1–2.

Petition, bringing ourselves and our needs to God. Remembering them and requesting things of the Lord for ourselves. Philippians 4:6 and Hebrews 4:15–16.

Thanksgiving prayers, that express gratitude to God for His specific blessings and gifts to us, 1 Thessalonians 5:18.

Praise, is expressions of adoration directed to God without the mention of ourselves or others, only God. We praise God by expressing words of honor to Him for His character, His name, His will, His Word, His glory, etc. 1 Chronicles 29:11–13.

When a man dates his wife-to-be, praise becomes an important part of courting. When he appreciates the beauty of her hair, he should express it to her verbally. He should compliment her beauty, her choice of perfume and clothing, and her excellent taste. If he enjoys her cooking or a special gift, he should freely express his appreciation. If he admires the way she expresses herself, again, he should say something. When you love someone, praise should come naturally because it's a genuine and stimulating part of a growing relationship.

Praise isn't really something we do for God because He has no ego to soothe. We praise God for what it does for us. David found personal satisfaction in expressing praise for the Lord. *28th July 2013*

I RETURNED FROM THE VILLAGE WITH EMMA. 29TH July 2013

IN A LIFE TIME I CUT MY HAIR. I FEEL HEAVY PRESENCE OF the Lord and Heavy intercession. I feel like crying inside me. 30th July 2013

I DRANK TOO MUCH CINNAMON AND HAD NO SLEEP.

DREAM, I WAS STANDING IN FRONT OF THE CONTAINER AND Sis Keren of Kiko was sitting down. The Heaven opened and I saw beautiful white and blue roses in a box. I shouted to Keren to look towards heaven but she did not see them. As the roses were disappearing a big Bible descended down with a scripture from Habakkuk, before it touched ground there came a helicopter passed by me to go and land in my beautiful flower garden, when I looked where it was going to land there appeared a group of Muslims dressed in white with white cups.

Under the helicopter were blades and by the time I realized it had landed and slashed all the Muslims to death and all what I could see were only white pieces of their tunics and the green grass.

As I was crying and wondering about the Moslems a dark tall man who looked he was from west Nile came my way holding a plaque and reported that the work is accomplished. I woke up.

Meditating on the goodness of the Lord, some time ago my

prayer was Lord here I am for your Take, for your Keep, and For your Use.

For your Take, in the world there is no one who is a friend, everyone does not like me because we do not speak the same language, we do not have same interest, we do not walk on the same ground whether relatives, clans people or even those whom I considered friends. So, take me keep me in your presence and use me till you return. Amen. *2nd August 2013*

SIN DOES NOT WAKE UP THE CHURCH, SO PERSECUTION WILL HAVE TO.

Their sinful ways make a mockery of the cross and cheapen its message. They support criminal and brutal leaders who bring harm on others and destroy nations. They lie, they cheat, they deceive, they betray. They rebel. They condemn and destroy. They ride the Beast, and the beast will destroy them. They bring persecution to true believers with their terrible scandalous ways that are publicized all over the media. Unbelievers think the true believers are just like the false ones, so they hate them all. *4th August 2013*

Message, A King will reign in righteousness and women of ease are warned of disaster, Isaiah 32.

I WORKED IN THE GARDEN WITH THE CHILDREN TO CUT AND collect the maize in the garden. *9th August 2013*

I worked with the children to remove the husks from all the heaps of maize. The boarding children left for holidays. *10th August 2013*

The English word "know" is translated into Hebrew as "yada." When used in reference to a person, it denotes a personal, experiential knowledge, and not mere recognition. (see Genesis 4:1; 19:8; Numbers 31:17, 35; Judges 11:39; 21:11; 1 Kings 1:4; 1 Samuel 1:19).

And Adam knew Eve his wife, Genesis 4:1,

two daughters which have not known man; Genesis 19:8,

every woman that hath known man by lying with him, Numbers 31:17,

of women that had not known man by lying with him, Numbers 31:35,

and she knew no man. And it was a custom in Israel, Judges 11:39,

woman that hath lain by man, Judges 21:11,

but the king knew her not., 1 Kings 1:4,

and Elkanah knew Hannah his wife, 1 Samuel 1:19.

Our knowledge of God should be personal and experiential, not merely theological.

And I will take you to me for a people, and I will be to you a God: and ye shall know that I am the Lord your God, Exodus 6:7.

Be still and know that I am God, Psalm 46:10. *11th August 2013*

CHAPTER TWENTY-SIX
THE ONLY FAITHFUL FRIEND IS OUR LORD

MESSAGE, King Hezekiah was such a king of Judah who trusted the Lord these are his encouraging words even if his kingdom was threatened by Sennacherib the Syrian. And he set combat commanders over the people and gathered them together to him in the square at the gate of the city and spoke encouragingly to them, saying: "Be strong and courageous. Do not be afraid or dismayed before the king of Assyria and all the horde that is with him, for there are more with us than with him. With him is an arm of flesh, but with us is the Lord our God, to help us and to Fight our battles." And the people took confidence from the words of Hezekiah king of Judah. 2 Chronicles 32:6-8 (ESV).

Then Hezekiah the king and Isaiah the prophet, the son of Amoz, prayed because of this and cried to heaven. And the Lord sent an angel, who cut off 185,000 mighty warriors and commanders and officers in the Camp of the king of Assyria. So, he returned with shame of face to his own land. And when he came into the house of his god, some of his own sons struck him down there with the sword. 2 Chronicles 32:20-21 (ESV).

Mannasseh, After the death of his father Hezekiah he

became a king, but evil, until the Lord let the Assyrians take him captive. He repented and the Lord returned him to his kingdom. And when he was in distress, he entreated the favor of the Lord his God and humbled himself greatly before the God of his fathers. He prayed to him, and God was moved by his entreaty and heard his plea and brought him again to Jerusalem into his kingdom. Then Manasseh knew that the Lord was God. 2 Chronicles 33:12-13 (ESV).

King Josiah son of Manasseh, Josiah was eight years old when he began to reign, and he reigned thirty-one years in Jerusalem. And he did what was right in the eyes of the Lord, and walked in the ways of David his father; and he did not turn aside to the right hand or to the left. For in the eighth year of his reign, while he was yet a boy, he began to seek the God of David his father, and in the twelfth year he began to purge Judah and Jerusalem of the high places, the Asherim, and the carved and the metal images. And they chopped down the altars of the Baals in his presence, and he cut down the incense altars that stood above them. And he broke in pieces the Asherim and the carved and the metal images, and he made dust of them and scattered it over the graves of those who had sacrificed to them. He also burned the bones of the priests on their altars and cleansed Judah and Jerusalem. 2 Chronicles 34:1-5 (ESV).

EVIL WAS IN-BORN.

Evil was in born. How did Manasseh become so evil when his father was so good? How did king Josiah be so good when his father was evil? He became a king when he was only 8 years and at 16 he took such a stand to clear idols which his father had left behind.

One can be born from an evil background but because the

Lord says that I knew you before you were born I chose you, even if your family has been so wicked the Lord will use you mightily for His Glory. Those days people never went to inquire straight to the Lord they had to go through the Prophets.

And when the king heard the words of the Law, he tore his clothes. And the king commanded Hilkiah, Ahikam the son of Shaphan, Abdon the son of Micah, Shaphan the secretary, and Asaiah the king's servant, saying, "Go, inquire of the Lord for me and for those who are left in Israel and in Judah, concerning the words of the book that has been found. For great is the wrath of the Lord that is poured out on us, because our fathers have not kept the word of the Lord, to do according to all that is written in this book." Josiah all his days did not turn away from following the Lord. And Josiah took away all the abominations from all the territory that belonged to the people of Israel and made all who were present in Israel serve the Lord their God. All his days they did not turn away from following the Lord, the God of their fathers. 2 Chronicles 34:33 (ESV). *17th August 2013*

I WOKE UP WITH THE THOUGHT OF HAVING NO FRIENDS AND I concluded that the only faithful friend is Our Lord. He is the one who does not leave us or forsake us. He is the one who sticks forever. Many people wonder and worry who will bury them when they die, because in the world everyone is an enemy.

The Holy Spirit brought this to me. Moses brought the children of Israel from Egypt, when they were about to reach Canaan land the Lord took Moses and showed him the land and told him that he will not reach there. Moses died on that Mt Horeb and the Lord buried him there, Himself without any children of Israel knowing where He was buried. Why should one worry about anybody coming to burry him or her, when the Spirit of God leaves the real person is gone to his or her maker and the body does not make any meaning, whether it is buried by one, group or multitude it does not matter. Some popular leaders like Osama bin Laden, the al-qaeda leader, Saddam Hussein of Iraq, Muammar Gaddafi of Libya were popular Moslem leaders, buried by one or two people who did not even want their graves to be known.

Many times people who go to bury go with real love, but the enemies go to establish that is that person really dead. Some go knowing that they will find so and so whom they haven't seen for some time, yet others go because they should be noticed that they also buried.

I was at a funeral when one gentleman was a nephew of the deceased when he stood to speak he said "I must confess I did not come here at all as I always pass by over there. I would not come here but I loved my aunt very much better than those who had kept coming to see her.

Really? Can one love someone you do not see, talk to or visit? On that same burial my uncle escorted the one who was chosen to speak on behalf of the mum's clan after she spoke, he did not want to leave without saying something. He took the microphone and said I am the uncle of the deceased but I do not come here. What I know he had never stepped in that yard until that day, but he did not want to leave without being noticed that he was there.

So, let us not worry about who will bury us, but let us continue building our relationship with the Lord. He is the one who knows the real friends who will bury us.

There are true believers who are real! Real! For the Lord living in China and Russia, in the underground churches, in prison confinements as Cori ten Boom book says her sister died in confinement, when they die they are not buried decently some bodies are cremated and some were thrown in mass graves.

In the time of Nero Christians were put on stakes poured kerosene and lit to give light for king Nero to be able to see his flower garden. Forget a decent burial with flowers, speeches and a big gathering, only ask to be a friend of God so that He will bury you Himself. *18th August 2013*

Visit to the US

CHAPTER TWENTY-SEVEN
THE RELIGIOUS SPIRIT

MESSAGE, The following "15 Signs of a Religious Spirit" are derived from the Book of Jude, and from Jack Deere's teaching Exposing the Religious Spirit. This list delineates a spectrum of expressions of the religious mindset. Manifestations of the religious spirit are not limited to Christianity, but can be identified in any false religion as well.

Characteristics

1. Rift - One with a religious spirit believes he has a mission to tear down error or what he believes is wrong. (what if he really believes it is wrong and it is?)
2. Rebuke - He has a hard time receiving rebuke from someone less spiritual than he.
3. Rebellious - He will not listen to people, because he can hear from God. (true)
4. Repulsed - He immediately notices what is wrong with people, or the church, rather than looking for what is right. (judgment spirit)
5. Rigorous - He keeps score on his spiritual life and

carries guilt when he doesn't add up to the Lord's standards.

6. Rejecting - He feels as though he has been appointed to fix everybody else. (leave them alone and they perish if they have to perish)
7. Rival - He may feel as though he is truly closer to God than others, and his life or ministry is more pleasing to God in comparison. (stop comparisons)
8. Ranks - He takes pride in spiritual discipline or spiritual maturity and ranks himself against others. (Fight the spirit of self ranking)
9. Reputation - He will do things in order to be noticed or affirmed by people. (keep low profile)
10. Rigid - Religious spirits are overly repulsed by "emotionalism."
11. Raucous - Seemingly converse to the prior, a religious spirit will use emotionalism or hype to manipulate people.
12. Resistant - He will tend to resist the supernatural or reject spiritual manifestations he cannot understand. (ask God if the. Manifestation is of Him)
13. Reactionary - He will overreact to carnality or immaturity in the body of Christ. (pray to God to bear and correct)
14. Renegade - He will not fully commit to a church or lend a hand to help if the group is not "perfect" in their theology. (we have to help them any way no one is perfect but other do not want to be helped)
15. Refrain - He will tend to be suspicious of or even oppose new moves of God. (we have always to be in the Spirit of God to be able to tell these days many cults are on the raise).
16. A Religious Spirit or mindset seeks to substitute

religious activity for the power of the Holy Spirit and the grace of God in the believer's life. The primary objective of a Religious Spirit or mindset is to have the church "maintain an outward form of Godliness," while denying the power of the Holy Spirit. This is accomplished by seeking to replace true repentance and grace with religious performance and works.

Also this knows that in the last days perilous times shall come. For men shall be lovers of their own selves, covetous, boasters, proud, blasphemers, disobedient to parents, unthankful, unholy, Without natural affection, truce-breakers, false accusers, incontinent, fierce, despisers of those that are good, false ... or one who foments strife. traitors, heady, high-minded, lovers of pleasures more than lovers of God; Having a form of godliness, but denying the power thereof: from such turn away, 2 Timothy 3:1-5.

This Religious Spirit can work in partnership with the Jezebel Spirit which is controlling, dominating and manipulative spirit! And Deadly! This spirit works together with the Witchcraft ... plain and simple! The Jezebel Spirit will always be found close to someone who carries the Elijah Spirit ... the Elijah Mantle!

They will show up in a circle of friends, Bible studies or at church and will do everything in their power to counteract the ministries their success and is to pull them down. They do not want you to succeed to minister the gospel, and especially to do deliverance and set people free! They are jealous of everything that you do! This religious spirit wants to keep us from hearing the present-day word by keeping us in the past reading the Torah instead of in the New Testament! Now, there is nothing wrong with the Torah! This spirit will quote scriptures or show you scriptures until the cows come home!!! They can't give you enough scriptures! You see them on your computer posts and in your comments. They take advantage of your posts and quote as many scriptures as they can to either support your claim or disclaim it! They not only will leave one comment but come back and leave another and yet another! They want to control Your Posts! They want all the attention instead of you! Their goal is to distract the others from the real topic! They want to get everyone off track, therefore causing confusion in the end, and they do!

The Religious Spirit also works through a Spirit of Pride and Haughtiness! People who operate with these spirits usually have a tremendous amount of pride! They so they think they are better than everyone else because "they know the word of God" better than anyone! They always trying and controlling the conversations by telling you endless facts why they are right! They never stop talking! They want all the attention in the room! They actually become obnoxious! To we who have discernment and they make us sick!

This religious spirit is under the Strongman of Lying, the Lying Spirit!

The spirits that are connected to this are: strong deceptions, flattery, superstitious, accusing spirits, religious bondages, false prophesies, gossiping, and false teachers.

Now if you have this Controlling Religious Spirit of any others:

Pray: In Jesus name ... (e.g. satan, etc.) ... I bind your powers this day and your religious spirits according to Matthew 18:18 which says Whatsoever I shall bind on earth shall be bound in heaven: and whatsoever I shall loose on earth shall be loosed in heaven!

So, I bind you now and your demons of: Religion; False Teaching; Legality; Religious Bondages, Pride, Haughtiness and arrogance; the Jezebel spirit, witchcraft spirits that are dominating, controlling and manipulative, gossiping and accusatory spirits, spirit of deceptions and lying, as well as superstitious spirits.

I cast them out! I put the blood of Jesus at the root at which they came in.

I close those doors and seal them with the blood of Jesus and I forbid them to come back in anyway, shape or form.

I send them to Jesus for judgment and they cannot touch anyone else on the way.

I loose now: Your Holy Spirit to the max, Lord, flush me out!

I loose your truth into my mind and my heart!

I loose love, joy, your mercy and grace, a desire to put others first instead of myself.

Forgive me for craving attention! Lord, fill the gap in my life! Fill me to overflowing with your Agape Love!

Lord, send out your warring angels now to defeat the enemy, to Fight and do battle for me in this area!

I call them forth Lord! Thank you Jesus, thank you for intervening! In Jesus name I pray.

Amen, and Amen. *20th August 2013*

I WOKE UP IN A PRAYER BATTLE JOINED THE RADIO IMPACT Mukiibi.

Speak to me Lord, I said with my random Bible opening:
Message,

God's promises and warnings to king Solomon after he built the Temple, 1 Kings 9; God is our protector, You are my God in You I trust, Psalm 91; The future of Jerusalem, Isaiah 60;

Good news of deliverance, Isaiah 61, 62;

God's victory over nations and His goodness to Israel, Isaiah's prayer, Isaiah 63, 64. *22nd August 2013*

CHAPTER TWENTY-EIGHT
ONLY YOU WITH YOUR LOVE

I WOKE up with the answer from the Lord as usual, it was from two songs:

> Comforter is who You are to me
> Peace Giver, Life Changer
> Joy River, Peace Giver
> Way Maker, Life Changer
> Peace Giver, Joy River
>
> COMFORTER BY CECE WINANS

Next, "God Can Make a Way"… where there seems to be no way by Don Moen.

The whole of 22nd August I was in such an attitude, asking myself so many questions.

Peter spent a night at home and still has no job. I had no money but I came back from the village with 500,000 usg the pickup truck got worse with the clutch plate, clutch pressure, nasals and later the battery. I spent all the money plus for the iPhones, and no money to work on it but working on my pick up. I decided to fast 12 hours and later malaria got me, Clare was trying to comfort me all day long. This day I was whining and complaining and counting scars from my past years.

Prayer, Lord, I work for no salary, Lord, also Clare works for no salary, Lord, Emma has no job, Lord, Peter has no job, Lord, Robert ran away, to where we all do not know, Lord, Amber House now the rent is to our neck, student registration is low, we are spending more than what we earn, and the land lady is demanding the rent for the house, Lord, we are bewitched by people that we did them no wrong! Amen.

I WAS REALLY WEEPING.

I was really weeping. For sure I was bearing the marks of a carnal month, week, day and I felt I grieved the Holy Spirit of God. So, before daybreak on the 23rd I came with desperation to change my heart when the Lord spoke to me through those two songs, one by Cece Winan and the other by Jaci Velasquez. I learnt from God and renewed our fellowship.

My failure has given me a sensitive, teachable spirit and has broken the pride barrier of my life and I was reminded of what Paul said Godly sorrow brings repentance that leads to salvation and leaves no regret, but worldly sorrow brings death, 2 Corinthians 7:10.

Thank you, Lord, for your message. *23rd August 2013*

ABOUT THE AUTHOR

The late Gertrude Kabatalemwa labored for the kingdom of God in her native land of Uganda. The burden of her heart was for the good news of Jesus to become deeply rooted, firmly grounded, and abundantly fruitful in the lives of the people of Uganda. In the past, she has served her nation as secretary to the president. She also functioned as Minister for the Development of Women.

At one point, she had taken in thirty-five of the orphans into her own village home, subsequently establishing Nyamabuga Foundational Schools for village children. Her plans include to prepare and equip these young people with the skills necessary to be able to lead their nation with a moral worldview.

Today, her children and those that she has poured into continue her work.

Through this book, you will be blessed by encountering the very large heart of this precious servant of God.

This is Gertrude's fifth book of the series "My Deepest Heart's Devotions."

facebook.com/neepuganda

www.ingramcontent.com/pod-product-compliance
Lightning Source LLC
Chambersburg PA
CBHW052145110526
44591CB00012B/1865